A Volume of
FORMAL NOTICES
from the
BUREAU OF COMMUNICATION

PUBLISHED IN 2010

TABLE OF CONTENTS

AN INTRODUCTION TO THE PRINTED VOLUME

In June of 1973, the Federal Bureau of Communication was closed due to purported budgetary cutbacks by the Nixon Administration. All the documents and files were seized and placed into storage, and the Bureau quickly faded from our collective memories. Over the past twenty-five years, little was known about this strange branch of government. We have been able to construct a piecemeal history of the Bureau thanks to the Freedom of Information Act and a fortuitous discovery of forms found in the personal effects of Morris Zuckerman, a collector of postal memorabilia.

Our recent efforts have sought to revitalize this essential piece of Americana, bringing it out of the archives and to a broader audience via the Internet and printed volumes such as the one in your hands. We are pleased to report that in addition to the classic forms, new Formal Notices are in development, and a new generation is discovering the value of written communication. In this era of digital communiqués, there is great value in reacquainting ourselves with the power of paper, pen, and the sincerity of the written word. Far from being a holdover from a bygone era, the revitalized Bureau sheds light on the human condition, keeping us honest with its constantly repeated mantra: "Let that which is unsaid be said!"

Wishing you clarity in your correspondence,
Your archivists:
Joshua & David Keay
New York, New York.

INSTRUCTIONS FOR USAGE

COMPOSE FORMS WITH A PENCIL

You would be well advised to compose your forms with pencil (or sharpened charcoal sticks) rather than pen, quill, or other implement. Oftentimes you will find that you have inadvertently conveyed the wrong message, and the forms are not designed to accept cross-outs or other forms of amendments.
Forms that have been written on cannot be refunded or exchanged.

PRACTICE EFFICIENCY OF LANGUAGE

Brevity, the sister of expediency, will oftentimes be required in completing these forms. It is to the benefit of both the writer and the reader to respect the natural language of the forms. Writers may find it beneficial to recall the timeless words of Cicero:
"Brevity is a great charm of eloquence."

USE PROPER HANDWRITING THROUGHOUT

The constrained proportions of the forms, dictated by postal code, have led to smaller writing areas. If you find that your words are requiring more space, please refer to the Bureau's pamphlet entitled *A New System for Written Communication*. For those whose handwriting remains less than optimal, a mechanical secretary, also known as a Type-Righter™ machine may be utilized.

REFRAIN FROM ALL ATTEMPTS AT HUMOR

Jokes, asides, and intimations all obfuscate the essential clarity of communication, which the Bureau holds as its highest virtue. Moreover, jokes are inherently regional in nature and often prove offensive to individuals of different sensibilities. Remember that an acerbic wit is always defeated by earnest honesty.

FIGURE 1 – PROPER PENCIL HOLDING TECHNIQUE

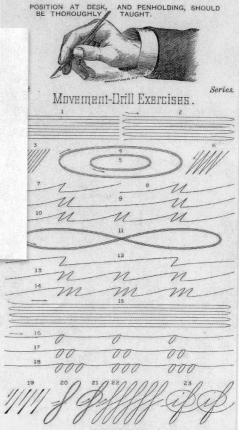

A sample of the proposed New American Standard Script

POSTMASTER WM. BARRY POSED FOR THIS
ENGRAVING TO DEMONSTRATE PROPER
LETTER FORMING POSTURE.

The Bureau's Penmanship forms were met with a chilly reception - the booklets, initially sold through post offices for five cents, languished for two years with few sales. When postmasters complained, forms were made free. Still, customers remained uninterested. In an effort to dispose of the surplus while keeping postal agents active, forms were mailed out to the general populace. Though the forms were finally adopted by masses, it is an ignominious footnote in Bureau history that the books were among the first pieces of unsolicited, or "junk" mail sent in the U.S.

THE EARLY YEARS

The Bureau, with its long and twisted history, has an appropriately curious origin. In the first half of the 1800s, a growing America required new communication technologies. To support the needs of industry, President Andrew Jackson enlarged the Postal Service. It was not a smooth process – difficulties emerged due to lack of infrastructure, employees, and transit technologies. Moreover, there were additional challenges. The largely uneducated populace had terrible handwriting, and tended to address letters with an undecipherable scrawl. At times, over a third of the messages were undeliverable due to the regional variances of handwriting. A man writing to his cousin had no assurance that the postal officer in the receiving town would be able to interpret the address and then deliver the message.

Thus, Postmaster General William Barry created the Federal Bureau of Communication in 1860, with the stated goal of unifying the regional handwriting styles "through a program of strict conformity." It was declared that the letter "t" should be taller than an "i" and that old style characters that would render "s" as "f" were to be banished. While early attempts at disseminating the information were less than successful, in time the new system gained widespread acceptance. The early Bureau shaped the handwriting of a nation, though its true purpose was yet to come.

Notes on Interacting with the Post Office

While the Bureau was originally founded as an offshoot of the U.S. Post Office, the two agencies have since parted ways. Regrettably, some animosity remains between the two groups, and while an uneasy truce has been declared, there may still be occasional flare-ups. The forms in this book have all been designed to comply with contemporary postal code, though in time, policies may change to suit the whims of belligerent postmen.

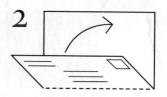

ALWAYS ATTACH SUFFICIENT POSTAGE. Regulations initiated during the Taft Administration dictate that for all pieces of folded mail, a proper first-class stamp must be affixed. While philatelists may harbor affection for Postcard Rate stamps, they regrettably are not as well appreciated by postmasters, who regard them as an anachronistic nuisance. Thus, use proper, full-rate postage, and affix it carefully in the correct orientation.

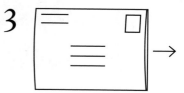

USE MINIMAL ADHESIVE, APPLIED IN THE PROPER LOCATION. The world of mail has changed dramatically since the era of the Pony Express. While humans are still partially responsible for delivering your mail, it is first sorted by a series of mechanical contraptions. Research has shown that machinery and cellophane adhesive tape are oftentimes at odds with each other. Place adhesive in the specified location on the form, or the Postmaster General may take note. While he is legally forbidden from reading your mail, he has many other ways of making your life miserable and it is best to avoid his wrath.

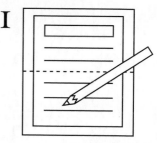

WHEN IN DOUBT, USE AN ENVELOPE. The Post Office's credo, which promises that your delivery will not be stopped by rain or snow or gloom of night, does not stipulate the condition of the message upon its arrival. As many have noticed, mail is often sullied and arrives marred with unsightly dirt, oil, and grime. To keep your Formal Notice in a condition suitable for framing, you would be well advised to encase it in a paper envelope, which will protect it from the elements and the filthy fingers of errant postal workers.

IN THE EVENT OF POSTAL FAILURE: *Do not express your frustrations to your local postperson!* They are a mere cog in the much larger machine, and oftentimes its greatest victims. Remember, your Postal Agent is an ally in the war with the greater bureaucracy.

SECRET ADMIRER
CORRESPONDENCE FORM

THE BUREAU OF COMMUNICATION

FORM NUMBER 12-22B

To My Dearest ....,

NAME OF RECIPIENT

....

DATE OF CORRESPONDENCE

First and foremost, I warn you — do not attempt to figure out who I am. My identity must remain a secret at all costs. Still, my heart is heavy and I must share my burden. I feel a great .... towards you. Ever since I saw you

ATTRACTION

...., I have known that you were different from all the rest. I do not wish to alarm you, but you should

PROVOCATIVE ACTION

know that I would stop at nothing to ...., even ....

DESIRED OUTCOME

CRAZY THING YOU WOULD DO FOR LOVE

That said, nothing would warm my heart more than to have these .... feelings reciprocated. If you are

ADJECTIVE

interested in exploring our love, please give me a sign: I propose that tomorrow you wear a ...., along with a

SPECIFIC GARMENT

.... in your hair. By this signal, I will recognize your interest.

STRANGE OBJECT

It occurs to me that you may not even know the extent of your interest, as I have not properly identified myself.

If I were to tell it outright, you will surely be shocked. So instead, let me tell you through a riddle:

I am the .... of .... children. My favorite color is .... and I oftentimes can be

[ELDEST/MIDDLEST/YOUNGEST]   NUMBER   BLACK OR OTHER COLOR

seen wearing .... My .... does this funny thing in the middle, no matter how hard I try to

A CONSPICUOUS ACCESSORY   BODY PART

fix it. I have .... moles on my face. My favorite song is .... and I prefer to write with a

A HIGH NUMBER   SEDUCTIVE TUNE

.... pen. I hate .... with a great passion. Kind strangers say that I bear an uncanny resemblance to

[BLUE/BLACK/RED]   REVILED PERSON/THING

.... If you somehow have not figured it out yet, my name rhymes with ....

HANDSOME CELEBRITY NAME   NONSENSE RHYMING WORD

Do not delay, send me a sign! My darling, our love awaits with a thousand imaginary kisses: ....

YOUR CHARMING NICKNAME

STEP ONE

WRITE THE NAME
OF SENDER HERE

STEP TWO

NEATLY WRITE THE
NAME AND ADDRESS
OF RECIPIENT HERE

AFFIX
POSTAGE
IN THIS
SPACE

THE BUREAU OF COMMUNICATION

BUREAU OF · COMMUNICATION
EST. 1860

FORMAL NOTICE

SECRET ADMIRER

REPLY TO ROMANTIC INQUIRY

STEP ONE: FILL OUT THE RESPONSE THAT YOU WISH TO DELIVER. CHOOSE WISELY; EMOTIONAL WELL-BEING IS AT STAKE.

GOOD NEWS

Dear Suitor ...., From ....
              LAST NAME OF RECIPIENT   NAME OF SENDER

I was/wasn't surprised to receive your request to
       CHOOSE ONE

.........................., and no doubt you will be
    PROPOSED ACTIVITY

happy to hear that I have good news for you: I would

be .... to spend time with you
         EMOTIONAL REACTION

.... Ever since we met, I have considered
    SPECIFIC TIME

you to be quite .... You strike me as a
                    COMPLIMENT

.... who would ....,
   RECIPIENT'S PROFESSION   STEREOTYPICAL TENDENCY

and I look forward to .... you.
                        VERB ENDING IN -ING

- [ ] One Question: What took so long?
- [ ] I must confess, I have a good feeling about this.
- [ ] A warning — I have nymphomaniacal tendencies.
- [ ] Perhaps you have confused me with someone else?
- [ ] Our age differences will not be a problem.
- [ ] I comply, despite my better judgment.
- [ ] You should know that I lack romantic experience.
- [ ] I think that we should keep this a secret.

BAD NEWS

To Whom It May Concern, From ....
                                    NAME OF SENDER

Regretfully, I cannot comply with your request to

.... While I am
    DESCRIPTION OF ROMANTIC SOLICITATION

flattered to be the recipient of your affections, I

regretfully cannot reciprocate them at the present

time. Frankly, I am too .... for you.
                           SELF-FLATTERING ADJECTIVE

Moreover, I consider you .... That
                          OPINION YOU HOLD ABOUT SUITOR

said, I wish you the best of luck in your future endeav-

ors. I propose that we just remain ....
                                    CURRENT NATURE OF RELATIONSHIP

- [ ] I am presently seeing someone else.
- [ ] I am of the wrong sexual orientation.
- [ ] We are affiliated with rival gangs.
- [ ] I am an unfeeling robot incapable of love.
- [ ] I am looking to play the field for a while more.
- [ ] I woul love to, but I'm really busy.
- [ ] We are politically incompatible.
- [ ] I would only break your heart.

STEP TWO: CUT FORM ALONG DOTTED LINE. | SEND ONLY ONE, DESTROY SUPERFLUOUS HALF OR SAVE FOR LATER USE.

THE BUREAU OF COMMUNICATION

FORMAL NOTICE

REPLY TO ROMANTIC INQUIRY

BUREAU OF · COMMUNICATION
EST. 1860

STEP ONE
WRITE THE NAME
OF SENDER HERE

STEP TWO
NEATLY WRITE THE
NAME AND ADDRESS
OF RECIPIENT HERE

AFFIX
POSTAGE
IN THIS
SPACE

OFFICIAL NOTICE
DECLARATION OF ROMANTIC FEELINGS

Bureau of Communication · Est. 1860

FORM ID: V-22

FILING DATE

STATEMENT

DEAR ...., I WISH TO INFORM YOU THAT
NAME OF RECIPIENT

I CONSIDER YOU TO BE A .... HUMAN
SUPERLATIVE

BEING, A QUALITY WHICH I CONSIDER ....
ADJECTIVE OF MAGNITUDE

ATTRACTIVE. FRANKLY, THE WORLD IS FILLED WITH

MANY .... PEOPLE, THOUGH YOU ARE
UNDESIRABLE HUMAN QUALITY

FAR MORE .... THAN THEM. I FIND
REMARKABLE CHARACTERISTIC

MYSELF DAYDREAMING ABOUT ....
PLOTLINE OF YOUR FANTASY

YOUR .... ARE LIKE .... AND
BODY PARTS (PLURAL) — *RARE OR PRECIOUS THINGS*

YOUR .... REMINDS ME OF ....
BODY PART (SINGULAR) — *SOMETHING DESIRABLE*

I WOULD HAPPILY ....
AN EXTREME ACT

IN ORDER TO .... I CAN ONLY
PURPOSE OF SUCH AN ABSURD ACTION

HOPE THAT YOU FEEL THE SAME ....
EUPHEMISM FOR ATTRACTION

TOWARD ME. I EAGERLY ANTICIPATE YOUR CANDID REPLY.

SINCERELY, YOUR ...., ...
RELATIONSHIP TO RECIPIENT — *NAME OF SENDER*

EXTENT OF INTEREST

CONFUSED — I HAVE A BIT OF A CRUSH — INFATUATED

○ ○ ○ ○ ○ ○ ○

I HAVE FELT THIS WAY SINCE

I WAS BORN — WE MET — THIS MORNING

○ ○ ○ ○ ○ ○ ○

SUGGESTED ACTIVITIES

GAZING	COPULATING
FLIRTING	BREEDING
CONVERSING	COHABITING
DANCING	KNOT-TYING
KISSING	GROWING OLD

PLEASE REPLY

IMMEDIATELY	IN WRITING
AT YOUR LEISURE	AND/OR IN PERSON
NO REPLY NECESSARY	WITH ENTHUSIASM

DISCLAIMER

THIS NOTICE IS INTENDED TO ALERT YOU TO MY FEELINGS AT THE MOMENT. FEELINGS MAY CHANGE RAPIDLY AND WITHOUT FURTHER NOTICE. IN THE EVENT THAT YOU ARE INTERESTED, ACT QUICKLY.

FURTHER NOTATION

PLEASE REFRAIN FROM THE USE OF POETRY

THE BUREAU OF COMMUNICATION

FORMAL NOTICE

DECLARATION OF ROMANTIC FEELINGS

BUREAU OF • COMMUNICATION
EST. 1860

STEP ONE
WRITE THE NAME
OF SENDER HERE

STEP TWO
NEATLY WRITE THE
NAME AND ADDRESS
OF RECIPIENT HERE

AFFIX
POSTAGE
IN THIS
SPACE

FILL-IN-THE-BLANK

UNIVERSAL LOVE POEM

RESULTS MAY VARY

BUREAU OF · COMMUNICATION · EST. 1860

SUNG TO THE TUNE OF "THE YELLOW ROSE OF TEXAS"

To My Dearest ...., From ....

You're more beautiful than ....

Or fresh .... and ....

More ....

Than Wednesday afternoon.

The sound of .... and ....

When you are ....

Reminds me of ....

In fourteenth-century France.

I miss the ....

When you are ....

I ....

Before I leave the house.

It wouldn't hurt to ....

Or ....

Just to let me know ....

Unless you've changed your mind.

PRINTED BY THE BUREAU OF COMMUNICATION, WASHINGTON D.C. USA. 1956

THE BUREAU OF COMMUNICATION

FORMAL NOTICE

UNIVERSAL LOVE POEM

STEP ONE
WRITE THE NAME
OF SENDER HERE

STEP TWO
NEATLY WRITE THE
NAME AND ADDRESS
OF RECIPIENT HERE

AFFIX
POSTAGE
IN THIS
SPACE

Fill-in-the-Blank
Pre-Nuptial Agreement

-For the Prevention of Marital Disaster-

To my Darling ...... [ENDEARING NICKNAME] ......,
Our recent decision to marry has me ...... [TERM OF ANTICIPATION] ......
over the prospects of starting a new life with you, and I can't
wait to begin our ...... [POETIC TERM FOR MARRIAGE] ...... Still, we must
remain realistic — we had separate lives before we met, and
down the line we might have a very good reason to go back to
them. If that ...... [EUPHEMISM FOR DREADED] ...... day comes, I want us to be
entirely well-prepared for it so we can handle it with as little
...... [DISCORD/DISMANERISM] ...... as possible. *First*, the easy
part: Anything we owned before the marriage stays that way.
There's no need to squabble over my ...... [IMPORTANT POSSESSION] ......
or your ...... [UNDESIRABLE OBJECT] ......, we both know whose is whose.
Second: Possessions we acquire whilst we are married. I
propose that we simply split them down the middle and call it
even. *Next:* Offspring. If this marriage goes as planned,
we're going to have a bunch of ...... [DESCRIBE YOUR FUTURE CHILDREN] ...... kids in
no time. We'll have to share them, so I propose that you raise the
youths during ...... [UNPLEASANT AGE FOR CHILDREN] ......, and I have them
...... [PLEASANT AGE TO BE WITH CHILDREN] ...... *Lastly,* there's the
...... [SORDID/DREADED] ...... topic of Money. All post-marriage finances
should be modeled after a ...... [COMMUNIST/DEMOCRATIC/TOTALITARIAN]
government, with ...... [YOU/ME/A LAWYER] ...... in charge.

Remember, my dear, I have every intention of staying with
you until ...... [OBJECTIVE OR METAPHORICAL TIME] ......, but if worse comes to
worst, this little agreement will surely help to put this whole
...... [SILLY/TEDIOUS/EXPENSIVE] ...... marriage business behind us.
May that day never come.

Th

....
THE WIFE

....
THE HUSBAND

....
PROFESSIONAL WITNESS

....
DATE AND TIME

STEP ONE
WRITE THE NAME
OF SENDER HERE

STEP TWO
NEATLY WRITE THE
NAME AND ADDRESS
OF RECIPIENT HERE

THE

FEDERAL BUREAU
OF
COMMUNICATION

EST. 1860

FORMAL NOTICE

PRENUPTIAL AGREEMENT

AFFIX
POSTAGE
IN THIS
SPACE

Marriage Proposal

TO MY DEAREST

Today, whilst pondering the _____ state of the human condition,
INCREDIBLY NEGATIVE ADJECTIVE

I realized we together have something particularly _____ .
UNIQUE/RARE/ENDANGERED

While most people are stuck walking blindly toward death, we have been given

the unique opportunity to rise above our _____ lives, and perhaps
BORING/MISERABLE/STUPID LITTLE

even experience a brief respite of joy in this horrible world.

What brought on these thoughts? I recently noticed that I cannot be away from

you without intense feelings of _____ , which serve only as a
A TERRIBLE FEELING

reminder of the _____ and _____ I am filled with when I am
FAR NICER FEELING _ANOTHER ONE_

by your side. Fortunately, my dear, I am quite clever, and have found a solution:

WE MUST WED AT ONCE!

We are perfect together; your _____ could not possibly
UNIQUE CHARACTERISTIC

compliment my _____ any more than the sky can hide from the sun.
EQUALLY ODD SKILL

Truly, by marrying, we will form a union that will serve as an example to all

mankind. Lesser couples will look toward us as a shining beacon of

_____ , and our _____ children will be the finest
POSITIVE QUALITY _NUMBER HIGHER THAN SEVEN_

examples of _____ known to man.
PLANNED PROFESSION FOR AFOREMENTIONED CHILDREN

If you too cannot deny the logic in this plan, meet me _____
REQUESTED CEREMONY DATE

at _____ and we will make it official. Do not delay!
CEREMONY VENUE

Then, We will Forever be known as:

_____ & _____

YOUR NAME _THEIR NAME_

STEP ONE

WRITE THE NAME
OF SENDER HERE

STEP TWO

NEATLY WRITE THE
NAME AND ADDRESS
OF RECIPIENT HERE

AFFIX
POSTAGE
IN THIS
SPACE

THE
BUREAU
OF
COMMUNICATION

FORMAL NOTICE

MARRIAGE PROPOSAL

A LIST OF Remembrances

DEAREST .... FROM ....

MEMORY, THE GREAT DECEIVER, WILL OFTEN TRICK US WITH FALSE TRUTHS, CONSTANT CHATTERING, REPETITIONS OF NONSENSE AND BLATHER THAT SEEK TO DISTRACT FROM THE NATURAL GIFTS AND VIRTUES ONE POSSESSES. MOREOVER, IN MY OWN EXPERIENCES, I HAVE SEEN JUST HOW READILY ONE CAN BEGIN TO TAKE ONESELF FOR GRANTED. THUS, I HAVE COMPILED THIS LIST AS A WRITTEN RECORD OF MY OPINIONS OF YOU. WHENEVER PLAGUED BY STINGING DOUBTS, I WOULD ADVISE YOU TO REFER TO THIS SHEET, CONVENIENTLY SIZED FOR EASY STORAGE. NEVER BE CAUGHT FAR FROM IT!

Let it Forever be Known

Your breath smells like wild ....

I have never met anyone as ....

Your .... is considerably .... than average.

I find your jokes to be funnier than ....

I would gladly spend the rest of my days .... with you.

Your hair is more .... than ....

When I am with you, time passes like .... to be with you.

If I had to, I would gladly fight ....

Since you came along, I am no longer afraid of ....

If I had a time machine, I would use it to ....

Your vocabulary makes me feel ....

I am happiest when you are ....

I still like you, in spite of your tendency to ....

This letter is the .... thing I have ever written.

A Final Assurance: NEITHER OF US KNOWS WHAT HIDEOUS FATES THE FUTURE HOLDS. IT IS POSSIBLE THAT IN TIME, THESE FEELINGS I HAVE WRITTEN MAY CHANGE. BUT LET IT BE SAID, THAT NO MATTER WHAT YOU OR I BECOME, AT THIS TIME I HOLD ALL THE OPINIONS ON THIS SHEET TO BE TRUTH THAT SHINES LIKE THE SHINIEST GOLD. I HOPE YOU NEVER FORGET. (WHICH IS WHY I WROTE IT DOWN!)

STEP ONE

WRITE THE NAME
OF SENDER HERE

STEP TWO

NEATLY WRITE THE
NAME AND ADDRESS
OF RECIPIENT HERE

AFFIX
POSTAGE
IN THIS
SPACE

THE
FEDERAL BUREAU
OF
COMMUNICATION
EST. 1860

FORMAL NOTICE

A LIST OF REMEMBRANCES

I, the undersigned, do formally and publicly offer forth this:

Declaration of Independence

When in the course of human events it becomes necessary for one person to dissolve the personal bonds which have connected them with another and assume their autonomous individual stations, decency requires that they declare the causes which impel them to separate.

Thus, I shall explain my motivations: While our time together has surely been beneficial for both parties, I realize that in order to pursue _____, I will need to set off on my own. My reasons are too plentiful to enumerate, so I shall record but a few:

First: I must be able to _____ without consulting with you first.

Secondly: I believe that the freedom to _____ is a right and not a privilege.

Thirdly: Your demands that I _____ are becoming increasingly _____ for me to comply with.

Fourthly: I wish achieve my goal of _____ which I fear I would never be able to do if we remain together.

Fifthly, and finally: You are not as _____ as you once were.

In conclusion, we chose to yoke ourselves together under our own free will, and I now choose independence using the same God-granted right. I respectfully request your compliance in the coming days, and trust you to maintain your steadfast character throughout. Godspeed, and farewell.

Sincerely,

_____

Relationship Emancipation form by The Bureau of Communication, Form Number 30-03857

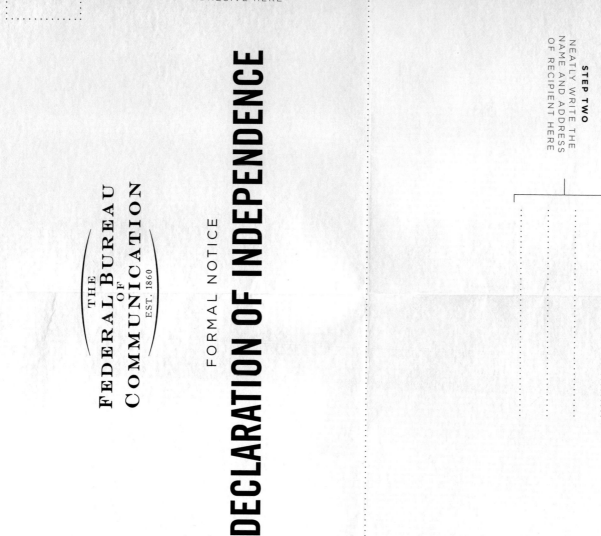

FORMAL NOTICE

DECLARATION OF INDEPENDENCE

THE
FEDERAL BUREAU
OF
COMMUNICATION
EST. 1860

STEP ONE
WRITE THE NAME
OF SENDER HERE

STEP TWO
NEATLY WRITE THE
NAME AND ADDRESS
OF RECIPIENT HERE

AFFIX
POSTAGE
IN THIS
SPACE

A WRITTEN RECORD OF REGRET

I FIND MYSELF WISHING FOR A TIME MACHINE. WHY, YOU MIGHT ASK? IF I HAD ONE, I WOULD USE IT TO .... (ACTION YOU WOULD HAVE TAKEN HAD YOU KNOWN WHAT IS NOW KNOWN) NO DOUBT THIS SOUNDS TRITE (MOREOVER, AN UNDULY OPTI-MISTIC ASSESSMENT OF MY ABILITY TO ALTER THE FLOW OF HISTORY), THOUGH IT IS UNFORTUNATELY TRUE. IT'S TAKEN LONGER THAN IT SHOULD, BUT I'M REALIZING THAT LIFE IS CONSIDERABLY HARDER THAN I HAD EVER IMAGINED. WHY WERE WE NEVER TOLD THAT .... ? (NEWLY REALIZED LIFE LESSON) I AM CERTAINLY OLD ENOUGH TO KNOW BETTER — SO HOW COULD I HAVE BEEN SUCH A .... ? (SELF-DEPRECATING COMMENT)

I DO NOT KNOW HOW TO PUT THIS (THUS, I HAVE RESORTED TO CORRESPONDING VIA FILL-IN-THE-BLANK FORMS), THOUGH IF I COULD TO EXPRESS MY FEELINGS IN WORDS, THEY WOULD BE:

I am so, so, so sorry.

MOREOVER, IF I HAD THE SPACE, I WOULD WRITE THE WORD "SO" ABOUT .... (LARGE NUMBER) MORE TIMES. AND I FEAR THAT EVEN THEN IT WOULD NOT PROPERLY DESCRIBE HOW I FEEL. NEED-LESS TO SAY, THIS IS A TRICKY SITUATION I FIND MYSELF IN.

THOUGH I HAVE ACCEPTED THAT MY TIME-TRAVEL WISH WILL MOST LIKELY NOT BE FULFILLED, I STILL HOLD ONTO HOPE THAT SOMEDAY THIS TERRIBLE SITUATION WILL SOMEHOW BE REPAIRED. I KNOW IT WILL NOT BE EASY, BUT I AM WILLING TO WORK FOR IT. VERY, VERY, VERY HARD.

SINCERELY, YOUR .... (HUMBLING ADJECTIVE) .... (ROLE), ... (NAME)

FORMAL NOTICE

A WRITTEN RECORD OF REGRET

THE BUREAU OF COMMUNICATION

STEP ONE
WRITE THE NAME
OF SENDER HERE

STEP TWO
NEATLY WRITE THE
NAME AND ADDRESS
OF RECIPIENT HERE

AFFIX
POSTAGE
IN THIS
SPACE

COLUMBIA TELEGRAM CORPORATION

CLASS OF SERVICE
This is a full-rate Telegram & Cablegram unless its deferred character is indicated by a suitable symbol above or preceding the address.

L.LUKENS PRESIDENT

B.ZHUK CORRESPONDENT

SYMBOLS
DL = D
NT = Overni
LC = Def
NLT = Cabl
Ship R

The filing time shown in the date line on telegrams and day letters is STANDARD TIME at point of origin.

ON MAY 24 1862
SOLDIER EDWIN MARSHALL DIED
APOLOGIES

END TRANSMISSION

US PATENT № 23445463

During the Civil War, the US Army used newly developed telegraph technology to break the news of the death of a soldier. After numerous incidents of outraged civilians, the Bureau was called upon to design a series of Telegraph Templates, which the operators could then fill in with salient details. The Notice of Fatality form enabled countless widows to receive their heartbreaking news with slightly more stylistic flourish than the earlier telegrams could ever permit. Thus was born the first Formal Notice, and the Bureau had found its true calling.

FORMAL NOTICE

Dear Bereaved,

We regret to inform you that *Edwin Marshall* has departed this dark world and gone on to be with his Maker.
NAME OF DECEASED

He died *bravely fighting in battle* on
MANNER OF DEATH

May 24, 1862 We thank you for
DATE OF DEATH

his brave service to *The State of Virginia*
DECEASED'S STATE OF ORIGIN

May our Maker provide you with a new

Brother even more *Clever*
ROLE IN FAMILY SUPERLATIVE

than the first.

Respectfully, *Sgt. Matthew Arlow*.
NAME OF SENDER

—— CAUSE OF DEATH ——

☐ Accident   ☐ Hubris
☒ Battle   ☐ Will of God
☐ Classified   ☐ Premature Autopsy

NEW TECHNOLOGIES & THE FIRST FORMS

Soon, the Bureau rose to a new challenge: A country divided. The Civil War was the first to utilize the newly developed electric telegraph. Speed of communication demanded a level of brevity that quickly proved to be unsuitable for conversation. The Bureau designed a series of Telegraph Templates, which the operators could then fill in with salient details while still presenting them in a readable fashion. Where before, telegraph style demanded awkward, preposition-free sentences, now the authors were free to communicate their news with greater detail and civilized style. An example, on the opposite side of this page: The Notice of Fatality form was created to allow the details of a soldier's death to be conveyed in greater detail, while featuring decorative elements which helped turn a simple letter into a treasured keepsake.

Simultaneously, the invention of the mechanical typewriter had rendered the original handwriting improvement mandate of the Bureau obsolete. Postmaster General Timothy Howe, a notorious paranoiac, became convinced that new innovations would render his beloved post office similarly unnecessary, and set into motion a plan that would preserve both his post office and the Bureau.

The Bureau was mandated to create a series of mailable postcards that could be filled out quickly and communicate essential information. Initially focused on invitations, requests, and business matters, the scope soon expanded to more interpersonal affairs such as apologies, grievances, and more. It is said that Howe was such a believer in the forms that he used them exclusively for all his correspondence. When he needed to express an idea that was not yet conveyable via form, he would simply commission the form to be created. Howe personally dictated the language in the Marriage Proposal and Last Will & Testament form. Thus was created the Bureau's most recognizable product, the Formal Notice. By the beginning of the 1900s, corresponding via the Bureau's forms was considered the height of fashion.

BUREAU OF COMMUNICATION
EST. 1860

AIRING OF GRIEVANCE

FORM G-7001

FILING DATE:

═ STATEMENT ═

TO: .... FROM: ....

NAME OF RECIPIENT   NAME OF SENDER

I AM SENDING YOU THIS MESSAGE TO ALERT YOU THAT I FIND

YOUR BEHAVIOR OF .... TO

OFFENSIVE ACTION

BE PARTICULARLY .... I WISH TO DRAW THIS

SENSATION

TO YOUR ATTENTION BECAUSE YOU MAY NOT BE AWARE OF THE

EFFECT THAT IT IS HAVING ON OTHERS. SPECIFICALLY, I FEEL

.... WHENEVER YOU ....

FEELING   DETAILS OF OFFENSE

AS AN ALTERNATIVE, I WOULD SUGGEST THAT INSTEAD YOU

COULD ....,

PREFERABLE ACTIVITY

AN ACTION THAT I WOULD FIND TO BE .... TIMES BETTER.

NUMBER

IF YOU CHOOSE TO PERSIST IN YOUR .... I MAY

OFFENSE RESTATED

HAVE NO CHOICE BUT TO ....

DIRE CONSEQUENCE

WHILE THIS IS ANOTHER POSSIBLE SOLUTION, IT WOULD BE

.... FOR BOTH PARTIES IF WE COULD AVOID IT.

POSITIVE MODIFIER

GRAVITY OF OFFENSE:

NEGLIGIBLE — MIDDLING — INCALCULABLE

◯ ◯ ◯ ◯ ◯ ◯ ◯

OFFENCE FREQUENCY:

	INCESSANT
	CONSTANT
	FREQUENT
	OCCASIONAL
	RARE
	ONCE
	NOT YET OCCURRED

SENTIMENT:

	THANK YOU
	SINCERELY
	MOST SERIOUSLY
	IT'S NOT PERSONAL
	RESPECTFULLY
	WITH LOVE
	WITHOUT LOVE

PARTIES OFFENDED:

	MYSELF
	OTHERS
	SOCIETY
	GOD

PLEASE RESPOND:

◯ NEVER
◯ IMMEDIATELY
◯ AT YOUR LEISURE
INCLUDE APOLOGY

═ ADDITIONAL NOTES ═

....

....

....

THE BUREAU OF · COMMUNICATION

BUREAU OF · COMMUNICATION · EST. 1860

FORMAL NOTICE

AIRING OF GRIEVANCE

STEP ONE
WRITE THE NAME
OF SENDER HERE

STEP TWO
NEATLY WRITE THE
NAME AND ADDRESS
OF RECIPIENT HERE

AFFIX
POSTAGE
IN THIS
SPACE

FORMAL APOLOGY

BUREAU OF · NON · COMMUNICATION · EST. 1860

FILING DATE

To: ....

From: ....

SINCERITY

HEARTFELT — BEGRUDGING — TECHNICAL

◯ ◯ ◯ ◯ ◯ ◯

STATEMENT

IT HAS COME TO MY ATTENTION THAT MY ACTION OF

.... COULD BE SEEN AS

BEHAVIOR WHICH YOU HAVE COME TO REGRET

☐ OFFENSIVE ☐ ANNOYING ☐ SELFISH ☐ HURTFUL.

I NEVER INTENDED TO ....

CONSEQUENCE OF YOUR ACTION

I WANT YOU TO UNDERSTAND THAT I WAS MERELY

TRYING TO ...., THOUGH I

YOUR INTENTION

CAN NOW SEE HOW IT COULD APPEAR THAT I WAS

.... PLEASE ACCEPT MY

PERCEIVED MOTIVE

.... APOLOGY. MOVING FORWARD, I WILL

ADJECTIVE

ATTEMPT TO .... THAT

PROPOSED SOLUTION

SAID, I WOULD VERY MUCH APPRECIATE IT IF YOU

....

REQUEST FOR OTHER PARTY

SINCERELY, YOUR ....,

RELATIONSHIP TO PERSON   YOUR NAME

EXCUSES

IT IS A HABIT.

I AM A NATURALLY SELFISH PERSON.

I THOUGHT IT WOULD BE FUNNY.

I DID NOT KNOW IT BOTHERED YOU.

YOU WERE NEVER SUPPOSED TO KNOW.

I WAS ☐ HUNGRY ☐ LONELY ☐ INTOXICATED.

IT WAS MY EVIL TWIN.

I FEEL ——— PLEASE

I FEEL	PLEASE
TERRIBLE.	FORGIVE ME.
GUILTY.	BE PATIENT WITH ME.
STUPID.	GIVE ME ANOTHER CHANCE.
SORRY.	FORGET IT EVER HAPPENED.
BLAMELESS.	DO NOT TRY TO GET EVEN.
VINDICATED.	DO NOT CALL THE POLICE.
BETTER NOW.	DO NOT TELL MY PARENTS.

ADDITIONAL NOTES

....

THE BUREAU OF COMMUNICATION

BUREAU OF · COMMUNICATION
EST. 1860

OFFICIAL NOTICE

FORMAL APOLOGY

STEP ONE
WRITE THE NAME
OF SENDER HERE

STEP TWO
NEATLY WRITE THE
NAME AND ADDRESS
OF RECIPIENT HERE

AFFIX
POSTAGE
IN THIS
SPACE

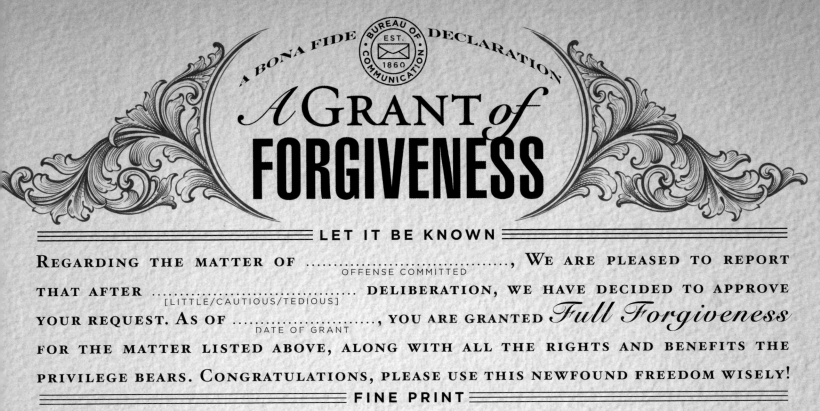

A BONA FIDE DECLARATION

BUREAU OF COMMUNICATION · EST. 1860

A GRANT of FORGIVENESS

═══ LET IT BE KNOWN ═══

REGARDING THE MATTER OF ...., WE ARE PLEASED TO REPORT

[OFFENSE COMMITTED]

THAT AFTER .... DELIBERATION, WE HAVE DECIDED TO APPROVE

[LITTLE/CAUTIOUS/TEDIOUS]

YOUR REQUEST. AS OF ...., YOU ARE GRANTED *Full Forgiveness*

[DATE OF GRANT]

FOR THE MATTER LISTED ABOVE, ALONG WITH ALL THE RIGHTS AND BENEFITS THE

PRIVILEGE BEARS. CONGRATULATIONS, PLEASE USE THIS NEWFOUND FREEDOM WISELY!

═══ FINE PRINT ═══

THE FORGIVENESS GRANTED BY THIS DOCUMENT IS NONTRANSFERABLE. IT IS VALID FOR ONLY THE OFFENSE EXPLICITLY LISTED ABOVE, AND ITS EFFECTS ONLY APPLY TO EVENTS THAT TOOK PLACE BEFORE THE DATE OF ISSUE. THIS DOCUMENT DOES NOT GRANT THE RIGHT TO REPEATED OFFENSE, EITHER INTENTIONAL OR ACCIDENTAL. FUTURE TRANSGRESSIONS WILL REQUIRE THE BEARER TO FILE AN ADDITIONAL APOLOGY APPLICATION FORM, WHICH MAY REQUIRE A SEPARATE REPEAT-OFFENSE FILING FEE. THEY WILL ALSO BE SUBJECT TO A PROBATIONARY PERIOD WHEREIN MATTERS WHICH HITHERTO NOW WERE CONSIDERED PERMISSIBLE WILL BE TREATED WITH GREATER PREJUDICE. THE DECISION TO GRANT FORGIVENESS WAS BASED ON NUMEROUS FACTORS, INCLUDING THE WEATHER AND EMOTIONAL VARIANCE, THUS, ANY FUTURE FORGIVENESS CANNOT BE GUARANTEED. WHILE ATTEMPTS WILL BE MADE TO REMOVE THIS EVENT FROM YOUR PERMANENT RECORD, SOME EVIDENCE MAY REMAIN. ALL ATTEMPTS TO NURTURE A FEELING OF TRUST WILL BE PURSUED, CONTINGENT ON A RECIPROCAL OUTREACH OF TRUSTWORTHY BEHAVIORS. DESPITE THE ASSURED ATTEMPT TO REMEDY THE SITUATION, DUE TO THE VOLATILE NATURE OF THE HUMAN CONDITION, IT IS POSSIBLE THAT THE RELATIONSHIP MAY NOT BE RESTORED TO ITS PREVIOUS STATE. LET IT BE KNOWN THAT IN SUCH AN EVENT, IT IS DUE TO EXTENUATING CIRCUMSTANCES RATHER THAN THE SPECIFICS OF THE MATTER AT HAND. LET IT ALSO BE SAID THAT YOUR ACT OF CONTRITION DOES NOT GO OVERLOOKED, AND SERVES AS AN EXAMPLE OF EXEMPLARY BEHAVIOR FOR AN AMERICAN. FORGIVENESS NOT VALID IN ALASKA OR HAWAII.

THE BUREAU OF COMMUNICATION

FORMAL NOTICE

GRANT OF FORGIVENESS

STEP ONE
WRITE THE NAME
OF SENDER HERE

STEP TWO
NEATLY WRITE THE
NAME AND ADDRESS
OF RECIPIENT HERE

AFFIX
POSTAGE
IN THIS
SPACE

STATEMENT OF GRATITUDE

BUREAU OF COMMUNICATION · EST. 1860

FORM **TY-009**

FILING DATE

TO: .... FROM: ....

═══ STATEMENT ═══

I WISH TO TAKE A MOMENT TO PROPERLY THANK YOU FOR

.... YOU
ACTION LEADING TO YOUR GRATITUDE

SHOULD KNOW THAT I AM .... GRATEFUL.
ADJECTIVE

YOUR ACTION SHOWS A MOST REMARKABLE LEVEL OF

.... WHILE LESSER INDIVIDUALS
VIRTUF OR QUALITY

WOULD HAVE MERELY .... ,
INFERIOR ACTION

YOU CHOSE TO ....
RECIPIENT'S SUPERIOR ACTION

I AM HONORED TO HAVE SUCH A ....
COMPLIMENTARY ADJECTIVE

HUMAN BEING AS A .... TO EXPRESS
TITLE OF RECIPIENT

THE TRUE EXTENT OF MY APPRECIATION, I WOULD HAVE

TO ....* WELL DONE!
EXTREME ACT OF GENEROSITY

SINCERELY, YOUR .... , ...
RELATIONSHIP TO RECIPIENT   YOUR NAME

*NOTE: THIS STATEMENT IS AN EXPRESSION, NOT A PROMISE, AND THUS BEARS NO GUARANTEE.

═══ EXTENT OF GRATITUDE ═══

EFFUSIVE — TEMPERATE — RESTRAINED
◯ ◯ ◯ ◯ ◯ ◯

CAUSE FOR GRATITUDE

◯ PRESENTATION OF A GIFT OR OFFERING.
◯ VOLUNTEERING ONE'S TIME OR ABILITIES.
◯ A SINGULARLY REMARKABLE ACT OF KINDNESS.
◯ AN ACT OF SELF-SACRIFICE.
◯ A PRIVATE DEED OF GOODLINESS.
◯ ONGOING ACTS OF VIRTUE.
◯ A REVERSAL FROM SELFISH WAYS.
◯

YOUR VIRTUES	I AM
BRAVERY	IN YOUR DEBT
PATIENCE	STILL SORRY
DISCRETION	CONFUSED
HONESTY	OVERWHELMED
PURITY	GOING TO REPAY YOU
CLEANLINESS	EXAGGERATING

═══ ADDITIONAL NOTES ═══

....

....

THE BUREAU OF COMMUNICATION

FORMAL NOTICE

STATEMENT OF GRATITUDE

STEP ONE
WRITE THE NAME
OF SENDER HERE

STEP TWO
NEATLY WRITE THE
NAME AND ADDRESS
OF RECIPIENT HERE

AFFIX
POSTAGE
IN THIS
SPACE

OFFICIAL NOTICE

UNSCHEDULED IMPAIRMENT

FORM **UW-77**

FILING DATE

BUREAU OF COMMUNICATION · EST. 1860

STATEMENT

TO: ....
NAME OF RECIPIENT

FROM: ....
NAME OF SENDER

PLEASE BE AWARE THAT I HAVE RECENTLY BEEN FORCED

TO CONFRONT THE SUDDEN LOSS OF ....
VALUED THING OR RELATIONSHIP

AS A RESULT, I HAVE BECOME ....
PRESENT STATE OF AFFECT

AND UNABLE TO .... I APOLOGIZE
EVERYDAY ACTIVITY

IN ADVANCE FOR ANY ....
UNFORTUNATE SIDE EFFECTS

TO WHICH YOU MAY BE SUBJECTED. BE ASSURED THAT IN

LIGHT OF PAST ISSUES WITH .... ,
REGRETTABLE BEHAVIOR

I WILL MAKE EVERY EFFORT TO ....
STATED GOAL

AND HAVE ASKED .... FOR ....
PERSON OR AGENCY   INTERVENTION

WHILE IN THE PAST, YOU MAY NOT HAVE UNDERSTOOD

MY .... FOR .... , I HOPE YOU WILL
FEELING   WHAT IS GONE

SHARE THE BURDEN OF .... WITH ME AS I MOVE
BAD THING

THROUGH THIS .... TRANSITION.
DESCRIPTION

THE CAUSE OF MY MISFORTUNE IS

UNKNOWABLE   INCOMPREHENSIBLE   OBVIOUS
◯ ◯ ◯ ◯ ◯ ◯ ◯

I FEAR LOSS OF:

- APPETITE
- INCOME
- BALANCE
- DIRECTION
- RESTRAINT
- MEMORY
- LIBIDO
- HAIR

I MAY REQUIRE:

- FORBEARANCE
- TOLERANCE
- FORGIVENESS
- AN AMBULANCE
- FRESH SEA AIR
- CLEAN SHEETS
- PAINKILLERS
- CASH

IN RETURN I CAN HUMBLY OFFER:

- ETERNAL GRATITUDE
- SOME OF THE MONEY I OWE YOU
- DONATION OF A KIDNEY OR CORNEA

SPECIAL REQUESTS
THANK YOU FOR YOUR CONSIDERATION

....

....

....

THE BUREAU OF COMMUNICATION

FORMAL NOTICE

UNSCHEDULED IMPAIRMENT

BUREAU OF · COMMUNICATION
EST. 1860

STEP ONE
WRITE THE NAME
OF SENDER HERE

STEP TWO
NEATLY WRITE THE
NAME AND ADDRESS
OF RECIPIENT HERE

AFFIX
POSTAGE
IN THIS
SPACE

REQUEST FOR
HEALTH IMPROVEMENT
WITH STEP BY STEP INSTRUCTIONS

THE
BUREAU OF
COMMUNICATION

FORM
DBM-T8

Dear ....,
NAME OF RECIPIENT

....
DATE SENT

Picture of health that you are, I must say I was a little surprised to hear that you are under the weather. It is truly a

testament to the poor state of this world when a .... person such as yourself comes down with
CONSTITUTIONAL QUALITY

a .... case of ....
GRUESOME ADJECTIVE   ILLNESS OR INJURY

While I've never personally been afflicted with ...., my .... is a ....,
NICKNAME FOR AFFLICTION   DISTANT FAMILY MEMBER   PROFESSION

and sends this advice: Firstly, you have got to keep a .... attitude. If you let this get the better of you,
[POSITIVE/HEALTHY/AGGRESSIVE]

then you will soon absolutely going to start having problems with your .... A warning: If you find
[SPLEEN/APPENDIX/GOUT]

that your .... starts turning ...., you should seek professional help right
BODY PART   COLOR

away. Once you have wearied of being ill, we have a secret cure in my family — you just have to .... a
VERB

.... twice a day. No matter how strange that may sound, it is guaranteed to fix you up fast.
NOUN

Lastly, if you are ever tempted to succumb to your illness, remember: Buck up! The world needs you. And I am sure

you will be back to your .... in no time and we will all try to forget that this ever happened.
STEREOTYPICAL HOBBY

Sincerely, your ☐ Coworker ☐ Friend ☐ Family ☐ Lover ☐ Doctor ☐ Undertaker ....
NAME OF SENDER

THE BUREAU OF COMMUNICATION

FORMAL NOTICE

REQUEST FOR HEALTH IMPROVEMENT

BUREAU OF · COMMUNICATION
EST. 1860

STEP ONE
WRITE THE NAME
OF SENDER HERE

STEP TWO
NEATLY WRITE THE
NAME AND ADDRESS
OF RECIPIENT HERE

AFFIX
POSTAGE
IN THIS
SPACE

UNFORTUNATE NEWS

MESSAGE

DEAR ....,
NAME OF RECIPIENT

HOW HAVE YOU BEEN? I'VE BEEN .... LIFE IS
POSITIVE ADJECTIVE THAT DOES NOT REVEAL NEWS

.... IN .... THE WEATHER HAS
[FINE/GOOD/GREAT]   GEOGRAPHIC REGION

BEEN .... I'VE BEEN ENJOYING
DESCRIPTION OF METEOROLOGICAL ACTIVITY

.... HOW IS YOUR ....?
SEASONAL FOOD YOU ENJOY   THING RECIPIENT ENJOYS

RECENTLY, I SAW A FILM ENTITLED ....
NAME OF A FILM

ALL ABOUT ...., WHICH I THOUGHT
BRIEF DESCRIPTION OF FILM

WAS .... I THINK YOU'D .... IT.
TWO WORD IMPRESSION OF THE FILM   [LOVE/HATE]

ASIDE FROM THAT, ... IS GOOD. I
[LIFE/WORK/EVERYTHING]

HAVE BEEN SLEEPING .... AND I HAD A
DESCRIPTION OF HOW YOU HAVE BEEN SLEEPING

FUNNY DREAM THAT ...., THOUGH I
BEGIN FORESHADOWING THE IMPENDING BAD NEWS

HAVE NO IDEA WHAT IT MIGHT SYMBOLIZE.

OH, ONE LAST THING: .... AND
FINALLY, DELIVER THE BAD NEWS HERE

....
CONSEQUENCE OF THIS UNFORTUNATE EVENT

THANKS FOR BEING SO ...., ...
POSITIVE ADJECTIVE   YOUR NAME

UPON FURTHER THOUGHT

- [ ] I SHOULD HAVE TOLD YOU SOONER
- [ ] IT IS NOT AS BAD AS IT SOUNDS
- [ ] YOU WILL GET USED TO IT
- [ ] AT LEAST I AM STILL ALIVE
- [ ] I AM AS SURPRISED AS YOU ARE
- [ ] WE SHOULD HAVE SEEN THIS COMING
- [ ] AT LEAST I HAVE GOT MY HEALTH
- [ ] I PROMISE I WILL FIX THIS

THE OFFICIAL STAGES OF GRIEF	YOU MAY ALSO EXPERIENCE
SHOCK	SURPRISE
DENIAL	DISAPPOINTMENT
ANGER	GUILT
BARGAINING	ANXIETY
DEPRESSION	NAUSEA
ACCEPTANCE	WRATH

CARRYING ON

I PROPOSE OUR NEXT STEPS SHOULD BE:

....

....

....

THE BUREAU OF COMMUNICATION

BUREAU OF · COMMUNICATION
EST. 1860

FORMAL NOTICE

UNFORTUNATE NEWS

STEP ONE
WRITE THE NAME
OF SENDER HERE

STEP TWO
NEATLY WRITE THE
NAME AND ADDRESS
OF RECIPIENT HERE

AFFIX
POSTAGE
IN THIS
SPACE

REVISIONIST HISTORY LESSON

▮▮▮▮ LET THE RECORDS SHOW ▮▮▮▮

Dear ....,

It has come to my attention that you mistakenly believe you caught me committing an unsavory act — ....
ACTIVITY WHICH NEVER TOOK PLACE.
Lest you think otherwise, let me assure you that you are mistaken. In fact, I was merely ....,
INNOCUOUS ACTIVITY
and any similarities to the former action were just imagined on your behalf. It is an understandable mistake, and I will attempt not to judge you for making it.

With that cleared up, it would be wise to remember how quiet I remained when I discovered your ....,
BAD HABIT
or perhaps the time you were caught ....
ILLICIT ACTIVITY.
A similar level of discretion in these matters would be most appreciated. If further untruths about my actions were to spread, I may be forced to ....
THREAT.
Please fill out the attached testimony receipt and return it to me promptly. Neither a threat nor a promise, ...
YOUR NAME

EXPERT WITNESS TESTIMONY

RECORD OF OBSERVANCE

I, ...,
NAME OF WITNESS
do solemnly swear that on the .... of
DATE
................,
MONTH
I witnessed the defendant going about the honest, fair, and legal business of ....,
PERFECTLY LEGAL ACTIVITY
and I am quite confident that he was not up to any malfeasance or misdeeds. Moreover, I can happily attest that he is an upstanding ....
NATIONALITY
and a very good ....
KIND OF PERSON
who I am sure would never even think of doing the terrible things that someone might misinterpret him as doing.

Sincerely, ...
NAME OF WITNESS

THE BUREAU OF COMMUNICATION

FORMAL NOTICE

REVISIONIST HISTORY LESSON

STEP ONE
WRITE THE NAME
OF SENDER HERE

STEP TWO
NEATLY WRITE THE
NAME AND ADDRESS
OF RECIPIENT HERE

AFFIX
POSTAGE
IN THIS
SPACE

I, the great ...., have gazed
into the far-off mists of time and beheld:

A VISION OF THE FUTURE
RECORDED FOR POSTERITY

Listen closely, dear reader, for what I am to say is of the gravest significance!

By the year .... , ... will have ....
FUTURE YEAR — PERSON, PLACE, OR THING — BEFALLEN A SPECIFIC FATE

Not all hope is lost, for .... will still be ....
SOMETHING MORE CONSTANT — PRESENT AND FUTURE STATE

What can be done to avert/induce this fateful future? By .... every
DIFFICULT HABIT OR RITUAL

day until .... , you may be able to .... this
IMPROBABLE EVENT — [ALTER/IMPROVE/IGNORE]

vision. But beware! If for some reason you do not heed my sage words of wisdom,

.... will befall you. And I will simply laugh!
AN EVEN MORE DREADFUL FATE

Let me assure you: I am so utterly confident in these assertions that if by some simple twist of fate,

they do not come true, I will happily I
ABSURD ACTION

dare make such a bold assertion because the future is so clear, it is as good as writ.

Form
Number
30-03857

THE BUREAU OF COMMUNICATION

FORMAL NOTICE

A VISION OF THE FUTURE

STEP ONE
WRITE THE NAME
OF SENDER HERE

STEP TWO
NEATLY WRITE THE
NAME AND ADDRESS
OF RECIPIENT HERE

AFFIX
POSTAGE
IN THIS
SPACE

Confessional Questionnaire

The Infamous European Parlour Game, Updated and Improved for American Sensibilities

All guests must complete a separate form and then reveal their humiliating secrets to the group. Laughter ensues.

1 What do you regard as the lowest depth of misery? ....

2 Where would you like to live? ....

3 What is your idea of earthly happiness? ....

4 Who are your favorite characters from history? ....

5 Who are your favorite heroes from real life? ....

6 Your favorite author? ....

7 Your favorite musician? ....

8 Your favorite artist? ....

9 The quality you most admire in a man? ....

10 The quality you most admire in a woman? ....

11 What quality do you most loathe in a person? ....

12 What is the favorite virtue that you possess? ....

13 Who would you have liked to be? ....

14 Your most marked characteristic? ....

15 What do you most value in your friends? ....

16 What is your principle defect? ....

17 What is your favorite occupation? ....

18 What would be your alternate vocation? ....

19 What to your mind would be the greatest of misfortunes? ....

20 What is your favorite color? ....

21 What are your favorite names? ....

22 What part of your appearance would you change? ....

23 At what time and place in your life were you most happy? ....

24 What is it you most dislike? ....

25 What natural talent would you most like to possess? ....

26 In what manner would you wish to die? ....

27 How would you describe your greatest fear? ....

28 What is your present state of mind? ....

29 Which is your favorite indulgence? ....

30 What is your motto? ....

....
NAME OF AUTHOR   AGE   DATE   SIGNATURE

"Turns enemies into friends, and friends into enemies"

Imported and Adapted Under the Wartime Entertainment Act by the Bureau of Communication. Form 20-34B4

THE
FEDERAL BUREAU
OF
COMMUNICATION
EST. 1860

FORMAL NOTICE

CONFESSIONAL QUESTIONNAIRE

STEP ONE

WRITE THE NAME
OF SENDER HERE

STEP TWO

NEATLY WRITE THE
NAME AND ADDRESS
OF RECIPIENT HERE

AFFIX
POSTAGE
IN THIS
SPACE

BELATED CORRESPONDENCE

FORM **Q-22**

FILING DATE

BUREAU OF COMMUNICATION · EST. 1860

MESSAGE

DEAR ...., FROM ....
NAME OF RECIPIENT   NAME OF SENDER

I HAVE BEEN MEANING TO WRITE TO YOU SINCE WE SPOKE

AT .... PLEASE DO NOT INTERPRET
LOCATION OF LAST CONVERSATION

MY SILENCE AS A STRANGE FORM OF JUDGMENT OF YOUR

.... RATHER, IT IS THAT I AM QUITE
[SOCIAL SKILLS/LOOKS/HEALTH]

PRONE TO SIMPLY .... OUR MEETING
PERSONAL FOIBLE THAT EXPLAINS YOUR SHORTCOMING

WAS QUITE MEMORABLE, I RECALL YOU MENTIONING

.... WHICH I REMEMBER AS QUITE
SUBJECT OF DISCUSSION

....
DESCRIBE YOUR REACTION TO THE CONVERSATION

☐ { I WISH TO CONTINUE OUR TALK, AS I FEEL THAT WE

COULD POTENTIALLY BE ....
[FRIENDS/LOVERS/CONSPIRATORS]

☐ { I HAVE A QUESTION REGARDING THE MATTER OF

....
IMPORTANT SUBJECT THAT HAS WEIGHED HEAVILY ON YOU

☐ { TO CLARIFY, WHEN I SAID ....
SOMETHING YOU REGRET

I ACTUALLY MEANT........................
WHAT YOU WISH YOU HAD SAID

SINCE WE HAVE SPOKEN

☐ I HAVE REMEMBERED YOU FONDLY.

☐ I HAVE MARRIED/DIVORCED/WIDOWED.

☐ I FIND MYSELF SEEKING EMPLOY.

☐ I HAVE HAD A CHANGE OF FORTUNE.

☐ I HAVE HAD TERRIBLE DREAMS.

☐ REGRETTABLY, LITTLE HAS CHANGED.

YOU STRIKE ME AS

☐	KIND	☐	TALENTED
☐	GENEROUS	☐	BEAUTIFUL
☐	PATIENT	☐	HONEST
☐	OPTIMISTIC	☐	CLEVER
☐	INTELLIGENT	☐	CHARMING
☐	BRILLIANT	☐	SIMILAR TO MYSELF

POSTSCRIPT

THERE IS NO NEED FOR YOUR REPLY TO BE AS SLOW IN COMING AS THIS LETTER WAS IN SENDING. INDEED, I CONSIDER PUNCTUALITY TO BE ONE OF THE MOST ADMIRABLE VIRTUES, AND CAN ASSURE YOU THAT ALL FUTURE MESSAGES WILL BE DELIVERED IN A MARKEDLY MORE EXPEDIENT FASHION.

THE BUREAU OF • COMMUNICATION

FORMAL NOTICE

BELATED CORRESPONDENCE

BUREAU OF • COMMUNICATION
EST. 1860

STEP ONE
WRITE THE NAME
OF SENDER HERE

STEP TWO
NEATLY WRITE THE
NAME AND ADDRESS
OF RECIPIENT HERE

AFFIX
POSTAGE
IN THIS
SPACE

ANONYMOUS ADVICE

FORM **TS3**

SALUTATION

Dear ☐ Friend ☐ Sibling ☐ Coworker ☐ Acquaintance ☐ Lover ☐ Stranger ☐ Roommate ☐ President

It is clear to me that the following conspicuous deficiencies may be impeding your advancement. To help you progress, I wish to inform you of the following areas for improvement. It occurs to me that you may be unaware of them, or unaware of other's awareness. We would be grateful if you were to rectify the problems listed below.

Please do not interpret my desire for anonymity as an insult; it is merely intended to ameliorate the awkwardness of direct conversation.

CHECK ALL THAT APPLY

☐ Your presence is distracting.
☐ Your sentences tend to run on.
☐ The plaque buildup on your teeth is visible.
☐ Your halitosis is unparalleled.
☐ Your punctuation appears unintentional.
☐ You've never said a positive word in your life.
☐ Your IQ is in the double digits.
☐ You lack discernment in friends.
☐ You chew with your mouth open.
☐ You lack sound judgment in cinema.
☐ Your deodorant is ineffective.
☐ Your spending is out of control.
☐ You lack self-confidence.
☐ You appear to need more sleep.
☐ You really should take better care of your skin.
☐ We all know you are involved with illicit substances.
☐ Your clothes are soiled.

☐ Your apartment smells curiously like garbage.
☐ You should read the instructions for the garbage disposal.
☐ Your time management skills are abysmal.
☐ Your accent is incomprehensible.
☐ You tend to eat with the wrong fork during dinner.
☐ Your contempt for me is palpable.
☐ Your music is too loud.
☐ Your casual swearing is not as charming as you may believe.
☐ Your vocabulary is pretentious and inscrutable.
☐ You too frequently mention your high intelligence.
☐ Your snoring keeps me awake at night.
☐ Despite your lack of class, you frequently display snobbishness.
☐ You need a haircut.
☐ Your nose hair situation requires attention.
☐ Your glasses are crooked and I cannot stop staring at them.
☐ I can hear your gum.
☐ I consider your monologues boring.

THANK YOU IN ADVANCE.

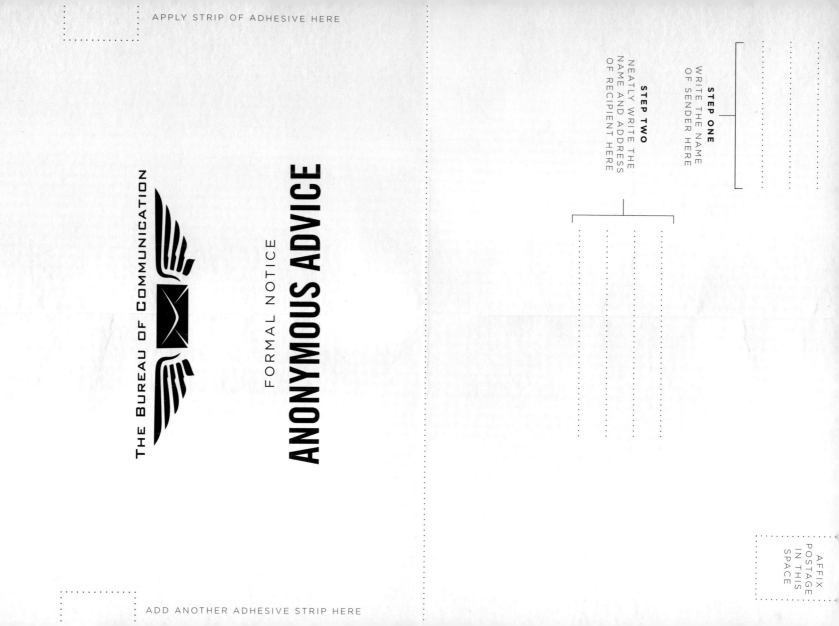

APPLY STRIP OF ADHESIVE HERE

THE BUREAU OF COMMUNICATION

FORMAL NOTICE

ANONYMOUS ADVICE

STEP ONE
WRITE THE NAME
OF SENDER HERE

STEP TWO
NEATLY WRITE THE
NAME AND ADDRESS
OF RECIPIENT HERE

AFFIX
POSTAGE
IN THIS
SPACE

ADD ANOTHER ADHESIVE STRIP HERE

Congratulations!

YOU HAVE DONE IT AGAIN!

I HAVE JUST LEARNED FROM .... THAT YOU HAVE RECENTLY
.... I WISH TO BE THE FIRST TO OFFER MY ....

SPECIFIC ACHIEVEMENT   POSITIVE ADJECTIVE

WORDS OF CONGRATULATION. WHILE YOU HAVE ALWAYS BEEN A ....
                                                            COMPLIMENT

PERSON, SHOWING OUTSTANDING MERIT IN .... AND ....,
                                          RECIPIENT'S TALENT   SKILL SET

EVEN I MUST ADMIT THAT YOU HAVE TRULY OUTDONE YOURSELF THIS TIME.

WHILE SOME MIGHT BE SURPRISED BY THE SUCCESS YOU HAVE ACHIEVED SO
........................, I MUST ADMIT THAT I HAVE SEEN THIS AS INEVITABLE EVER SINCE

MANNER OF ACHIEVEMENT

THE DAY YOU .... OTHERS MIGHT CALL YOUR GOOD FORTUNE
                        EARLY ACCOMPLISHMENT

THE PRODUCT OF LUCK, THOUGH I CAN CLEARLY SEE THAT IT IS THE RESULT OF
.... IN THIS TIME OF GREAT CELEBRATION, BE SURE TO TAKE A

VIRTUE WHICH MADE ACHIEVEMENT POSSIBLE.

MOMENT TO REFLECT BACK ON YOUR ...., AND APPRECIATE THE
                                          [BENEFACTORS / OLD FRIENDS / ENEMIES]

.... HEIGHTS YOU HAVE REACHED!
[STRATOSPHERIC / DANGEROUS]

WITH ☐LOVE, ☐ADMIRATION, ☐PRIDE, ☐HUMILITY, ☐RESPECT, ☐ENVY,

....
SIGNATURE OF SENDER

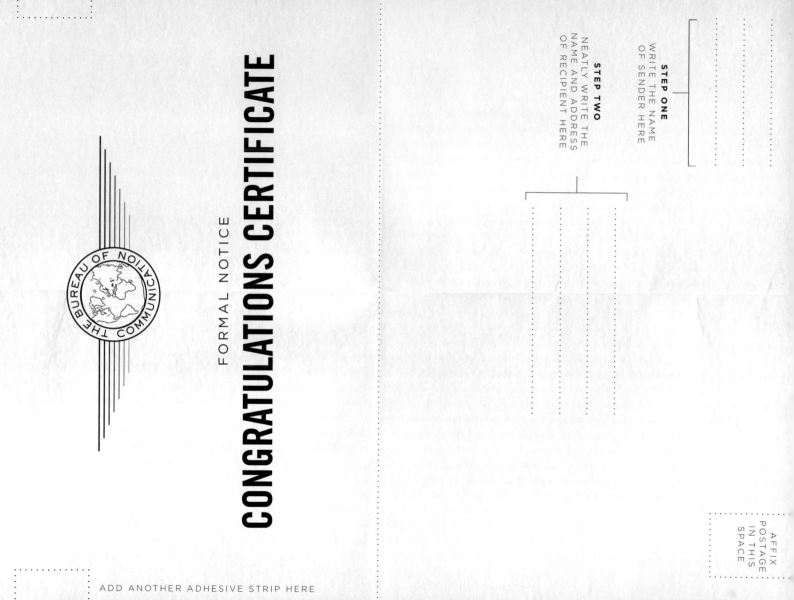

FORMAL NOTICE

CONGRATULATIONS CERTIFICATE

THE BUREAU OF COMMUNICATION

STEP ONE
WRITE THE NAME
OF SENDER HERE

STEP TWO
NEATLY WRITE THE
NAME AND ADDRESS
OF RECIPIENT HERE

AFFIX
POSTAGE
IN THIS
SPACE

BUREAU OF COMMUNICATION
EST. 1860

MESSAGE

DEAR ☐ FRIENDS ☐ FAMILY ☐ OTHER .... ,

ONCE AGAIN, ... IS UPON US. IN
NAME OF HOLIDAY OR SEASON

THIS MODERN WORLD, IT IS EASY THINK THE HOLIDAY IS

ONLY ABOUT .... AND .... ;
STEREOTYPICAL ACTIVITY   *CLICHE*

THOUGH IT IS IMPORTANT TO REMEMBER THE TRUE

MEANING: ....
HOLIDAY'S OFFICIAL RELIGIOUS OR POLITICAL SIGNIFICANCE

THAT SAID, HERE'S HOPING THAT YOU CAN SPEND A

LITTLE TIME .... , CATCH UP ON
PLEASANT ACTIVITY

SOME .... , AND GET TO EAT PLENTY
BIOLOGICAL NEED

OF .... WISHING YOU A VERY
TRADITIONAL FOOD

.... HOLIDAY. .... , ...
ADJECTIVE   *SALUTATION*   *NAME OF SENDER*

ADDITIONAL STATEMENT
BREVITY IS A VIRTUE

....

....

OCCASION

◯ THURSDAY	◯ INDEPENDENCE DAY
◯ GROUNDHOG DAY	◯ ROSH HASHANAH
◯ SUPER BOWL SUNDAY	◯ COLUMBUS DAY
◯ VALENTINE'S DAY	◯ HALLOWEEN
◯ CHINESE NEW YEAR	◯ DAY OF THE DEAD
◯ ST. PATRICK'S DAY	◯ VETERAN'S DAY
◯ APRIL FOOL'S DAY	◯ THANKSGIVING DAY
◯ PASSOVER	◯ HANUKKAH
◯ EASTER	◯ FESTIVUS
◯ CINCO DE MAYO	◯ CHRISTMAS
◯ MOTHER'S DAY	◯ KWANZAA
◯ MEMORIAL DAY	◯ NEW YEAR'S DAY
◯ FATHER'S DAY	◯ ....

SENTIMENT

☐ MAY YOUR NEXT YEAR BE BETTER THAN LAST.
☐ HAS IT BEEN ANOTHER YEAR, ALREADY?
☐ WHERE DID YOU GO/WHAT ARE YOU DOING?
☐ WE ANTICIPATE A GENEROUS GIVING SEASON.
☐ THERE IS SOMETHING WE HAVE TO DISCUSS.
☐ APOLOGIES ABOUT THE INCIDENT.
☐ REMEMBER TO DRINK PLENTY OF WATER.
☐ THIS CARD IS A MEANINGLESS FORMALITY.
☐ REGARDS.

THE BUREAU OF COMMUNICATION

FORMAL NOTICE

OBSERVANCE OF HOLIDAY

BUREAU OF · COMMUNICATION
EST. 1860

STEP ONE
WRITE THE NAME
OF SENDER HERE

STEP TWO
NEATLY WRITE THE
NAME AND ADRESS
OF RECIPIENT HERE

AFFIX
POSTAGE
IN THIS
SPACE

FORMAL STATEMENT
OFFICIAL INVITATION

BUREAU OF COMMUNICATION · EST. 1860

TO: .... FROM: ....
　　NAME OF RECIPIENT　　　　　NAME OF SENDER

DEAR ...., YOUR PRESENCE IS REQUESTED AT
　　RELATIONSHIP TO RECIPIENT

.... IT IS SURE TO BE
　　　　　EVENT

A .... EVENT, AND WE WOULD
　　　MODIFIER

BE .... TO HAVE YOU PARTICIPATE. WE
　　EMOTION

PLAN A GREAT DEAL OF ....
　　　　　　　　　　　　　　ACTIVITY

AND ...., THOUGH
　　ADDITIONAL ACTIVITY

WE DO NOT INTEND TO ....
　　　　　　　　UNPLANNED ACTIVITY

IF THAT IS A REQUIREMENT, YOU MAY WISH TO PURSUE

OTHER OPPORTUNITIES. WE AWAIT YOUR RESPONSE.

═ CRUCIAL DETAILS ═

..............., ... / .... / ...... @ ....
DAY OF THE WEEK　　MONTH　DAY　YEAR　　START TIME

....
　　　　　LOCATION + ADDRESS

....
　　　　　ADDITIONAL NOTES

PLANS INCLUDE:

- [ ] GRAZING
- [ ] FEASTING
- [ ] ALCOHOL
- [ ] DEBAUCHERY
- [ ] MUSIC
- [ ] CINEMA & GAMING
- [ ] FEATS OF STRENGTH
- [ ] ....

DRESS CODE:

- ( ) COSTUME
- ( ) BLACK TIE
- ( ) INTIMATE
- ( ) DANCEWEAR
- ( ) SWIMWEAR
- ( ) PROFESSIONAL
- ( ) COME AS YOU ARE
- [ ] *To Be Enforced*

PLEASE BRING:

- [ ] SUSTENANCE
- [ ] INTOXICANTS
- [ ] ASSOCIATES
- [ ] ....

KINDLY:

- [ ] *R.S.V.P.*
- [ ] *Be Punctual*
- [ ] *Tell No One*
- [ ] *Come Alone*

YOUR ABSENCE WOULD BE:

UNFORGIVABLE — CONSPICUOUS — PREFERABLE
( ) ( ) ( ) ( ) ( ) ( ) ( )

─ FINE PRINT ─

THE BUREAU OF · COMMUNICATION

FORMAL NOTICE

OFFICIAL INVITATION

BUREAU OF · COMMUNICATION
EST. 1860

STEP ONE
WRITE THE NAME
OF SENDER HERE

STEP TWO
NEATLY WRITE THE
NAME AND ADDRESS
OF RECIPIENT HERE

AFFIX
POSTAGE
IN THIS
SPACE

BUREAUCRATIC STATIONERY
RESCHEDULING REQUEST

FORM **F-99**

FILING DATE

MESSAGE

DEAR ☐ FRIEND ☐ LOVER ☐ PROFESSOR ☐ JUDGE,

TODAY, I WAS TRYING TO ....
OBLIGATION THAT MUST BE FULFILLED

BUT FOUND MYSELF WHOLLY DISTRACTED BY THE

MEMORY OF YOUR .... • I FOUND
MEMORABLE CHARACTERISTIC

IT HARD NOT TO .... WHEN I
ENTHUSIASTIC BEHAVIOR

THOUGHT OF OUR PLAN TO ....•
ANTICIPATED ACTIVITY

AND THUS, I FEAR I MUST POLITELY REQUEST THAT WE

POSTPONE OUR APPOINTMENT. UNDERSTAND THAT IT IS

NOT FOR A LACK OF WANTING TO SEE YOU, BUT TRULY THE

OPPOSITE — I AM AFRAID THAT IF I SEE YOU BEFORE I

............................., I WILL BECOME TOO
GOAL OF OBLIGATED ACTIVITY

.... BY YOU AND NEVER FIND THE
SIDE-EFFECT OF ACTIVITY PARTNER

WILLPOWER TO RETURN TO MY DUTIES.

THE GRACE AND GENEROSITY OF YOUR FORBEARANCE

WILL NOT SOON BE FORGOTTEN. SINCERELY, ...
SENDER'S INITIALS

A MODEST PROPOSAL

FORTUNATELY, FOR US AND OUR

............................., I WILL BE
NATURE OF RELATIONSHIP

AGAIN FREE TO ....
[MEET/PLAN/FIGHT]

WITH YOU ON ....•
DATE OF AVAILABILITY

I DO LOOK FORWARD TO FINALLY

.... WITH YOU THEN.
VERB ENDING IN -ING

MY LEVEL OF ANTICIPATION

INDIFFERENT	MODERATE	TREMENDOUS
○—○	○—○	○

I WISH TO MEET

POSTHASTE	SOON	THE HAZY FUTURE
○—○	○—○	○

AN ASSURANCE

☐ MY WORK IS FOR THE BETTERMENT OF MANKIND.
☐ I ALSO ABSTAIN FROM OTHER HUMAN CONTACT.
☐ MY DELAY IS NOT DUE TO A LACK OF AFFECTION.
☐ I HOLD YOUR TIME IN THE HIGHEST REGARD.
☐ I WANT TO OFFER YOU MY FULLEST ATTENTION.
☐ I CONSIDER "DISTRACTING" TO BE A COMPLIMENT.

THE BUREAU OF · COMMUNICATION

FORMAL NOTICE

RESCHEDULING REQUEST

BUREAU OF · COMMUNICATION
EST. 1860

STEP ONE
WRITE THE NAME
OF SENDER HERE

STEP TWO
NEATLY WRITE THE
NAME AND ADDRESS
OF RECIPIENT HERE

AFFIX
POSTAGE
IN THIS
SPACE

A CONTRACT WITH SELF

Upon reflecting back on my previous year, I have concluded that I must make some changes to my life. They include, but are not limited to:

DIET

I will eat far fewer .... , and imbibe less ....
DELICIOUS THINGS   EUPHEMISM FOR INTOXICANTS

Instead, I will dedicate myself to a daily regiment of ....
BORING FOOD

prepared only with .... Moreover, I will tend to my body by
FLAVORLESS SUBSTANCE

.... daily, without fail. Soon I will be nice and ....
TEDIOUS EXHAUSTING ACTIVITY   THIN/BORED

MEDIA

After perusing my bookshelves, it is clear that I have consumed too much

.... when I should have been ....
INDULGENT MEDIA   PREFERABLE ACTIVITY, -ING

Henceforth, I will double my efforts to purge my mind of the influence of

this rubbish and enrich my soul by taking in more ....
SUPERIOR MEDIA

WORK

I am sick of not having enough ...., so I resolve to save
[TIME/MONEY]

.... which will in turn get me more ....
[TIME/MONEY]   [TIME/MONEY]

I will invest .... only in things that matter.
[TIME/MONEY]

GROWTH

I'm sure that when I achieve these goals, I will be a ....
ADJECTIVE

person, who will feel less .... and never have to ....
NEGATIVE FEELING   BAD HABIT

I will soon accomplish it with the grace of a ....
AN ELEGANT ANIMAL

RELATIONSHIPS

It's clear that I've been spending too much time with ....
NAME OF STUPID FRIEND

which has caused my relationships with .... to whither.
GENDER YOU ARE SEXUALLY ATTRACTED TO

From here forward, I resolve to associate only with .... and
IMPRESSIVE FRIEND CATEGORY

........................, and not return the calls of my old friends.
RESPECTABLE PROFESSION

A WAGER

As I am confident in my ability to self improve, I would like to place a little

wager upon it. If I succeed in achieving these goals, I will have earned the

privilege to .... And in the unlikely event that I fall short of
INDULGENT REWARD

my ambition, I will .... and redouble my efforts next year.
INCONSEQUENTIAL CONSEQUENCE

SIGNED, THIS .... DAY OF ...., BY ...., A PERSON OF SOUND MIND AND JUDGMENT

APPLY STRIP OF ADHESIVE HERE

THE BUREAU OF COMMUNICATION

FORMAL NOTICE

NEW YEAR'S RESOLUTIONS

STEP ONE
WRITE THE NAME
OF SENDER HERE

STEP TWO
NEATLY WRITE THE
NAME AND ADDRESS
OF RECIPIENT HERE

AFFIX
POSTAGE
IN THIS
SPACE

ADD ANOTHER ADHESIVE STRIP HERE

Last Will & Testament

DEAREST FRIENDS, FAMILY, AND COURT OFFICIALS:

In the event that you are reading this, I have departed this mortal coil for the last time. DO NOT DESPAIR. I only hope that I died as I lived, and that you will remember me for

_____ and a _____. As a reward for being
REQUESTED MEMORY   SIGNIFICANT ROLE

_____, I bequest my _____ to _____
COMPLIMENT   GIFT   RECIPIENT NAME

Do not take this lightly — know that it is my most valued possession and I wish for you to care for it as if I am still alive inside of it! Give my _____ to _____,
ADDITIONAL GIFT   OTHER RECIPIENT

and have _____ **sort out what to do with the rest.**
RESPONSIBLE PERSON OR INSTITUTION

One more messy matter — what shall be done with my mortal remains? If even a glimmer of my former radiance shines on, please _____ my body and place it
REQUESTED PRESERVATION/DISPOSAL TECHNIQUE

_____, please **If this proves too** _____, please
CADAVER STORAGE LOCATION   ADVERB

donate me to _____. I'm sure they will
INSTITUTION, PHILANTHROPY, OR BUSINESS

think of something _____ **to do with me.**
[NOBLE/PROFITABLE/SURPRISING]

While I still have your attention, let me share with you this bit of advice: Always _____, and never let
SAGE ADVICE

anyone _____ your _____. Also,
VERB   NOUN

you'll find _____ hidden in _____.
SECRET THING   EXOTIC LOCATION

I always meant to tell you about that, but it never came up.

I love you all, _____
SIGNATURE OF DECEASED

Witness: _____
NAME OF TRUSTED ADVISOR

THE
BUREAU
OF
COMMUNICATION

FORMAL NOTICE

LAST WILL AND TESTAMENT

STEP ONE

WRITE THE NAME
OF SENDER HERE

STEP TWO

NEATLY WRITE THE
NAME AND ADDRESS
OF RECIPIENT HERE

AFFIX
POSTAGE
IN THIS
SPACE

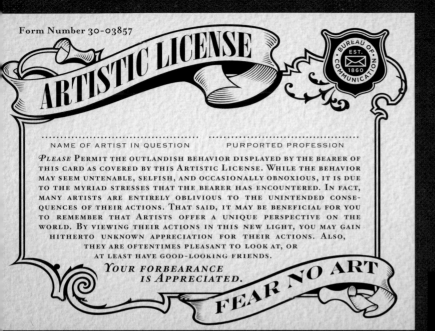

ARTISTIC LICENSE

The license forms on this page are two of the more curious findings from the Bureau archive. While their true significance is lost to the ages, we assume that they were created for humorous purposes. It is known that the Bureau's resident artists would use the equipment and facilities of the Bureau of Engraving and Printing for their own purposes. Most famous was an incident involving the fabrication of counterfeit bills. While it was argued that the forged bills were created for entertainment (a claim justified by the fact that they bore the portrait Charlie Chaplin), some bills did enter circulation and are now an elusive and prized addition to any numismatic's collection.

LICENSE TO KILL

While there is some evidence that the Bureau did provide its services to the War Department, one can infer that the License to Kill is not a legitimate form of identification. There is no record of the "Alliance of International Governing Bodies" anywhere in the National Archives, and all inquiries toward it have been met with a stony silence. Surely, the logistics of organizing a secret international society would preclude its existence. Moreover, the blanks on the form are filled with solid black. If such a license were ever to be issued, what pen could inscribe a name in such a space? The mere idea of such a document is preposterous, and therefore we must assume that anyone who believes in the legitimacy of such a form is the victim of a joke played upon history.

Artistic
License

NON TRANSFERABLE

Exitus Acta Probat

BUREAU OF COMMUNICATION · EST. 1860

OFFICIAL NOTICE

ACKNOWLEDGEMENT OF OCCASION

FORM **G-26**

FILING DATE:

STATEMENT

DEAR ....,
NAME OF RECIPIENT

IT HAS RECENTLY COME TO MY ATTENTION THAT YOU

WILL SOON BE OBSERVING ....•
EVENT

THIS IS A .... OCCASION. I PROPOSE YOU
ADJECTIVE

SHOULD COMMEMORATE THIS .... TIME BY
ADJECTIVE

....•. IT IS NOT EVERY DAY
SUGGESTED ACTIVITY

THAT ONE HAS A CHANCE TO ....•
CONSEQUENCE OF SUGGESTED ACTIVITY

I HOPE THAT YOU FEEL VERY ....•
SENSATION

WISHING YOU ....!
SENTIMENT

YOUR ...., ...
ADJECTIVE   RELATIONSHIP TO PERSON   YOUR NAME

ADDITIONAL NOTES
BREVITY IS A VIRTUE

....

....

....

OCCASION:

- ☐ Quinceaños
- ☐ Engagement
- ☐ Wedding
- ☐ Anniversary
- ☐ Divorce
- ☐ Birthday
- ☐ Bar Mitzvah
- ☐ First Communion
- ☐ National Holiday
- ☐ Fictional Holiday
- ☐ Graduation
- ☐ Life-alteration
- ....

MESSAGE SENT:

- ☐ Ahead of time
- ☐ Just in time
- ☐ Past due

ATTACHMENTS:

- ☐ Love
- ☐ Gifts
- ☐ Cash
- ☐ *Thanks Requested*

PLEASE REPLY:

- ◯ Never
- ◯ Immediately
- ◯ At your leisure

SIGNIFICANCE OF EVENT

Forgettable — Notable — Life changing
◯ ◯ ◯ ◯ ◯ ◯ ◯

SINCERITY OF SENTIMENT

Bona Fide – Honest – Simulated – Artificial
◯ ◯ ◯ ◯ ◯ ◯ ◯

DISCLAIMER

THE SENDER DENIES ANY RESPONSIBILITY FOR THE CONSEQUENCES OF SUGGESTED ACTIVITY.

THE BUREAU OF · COMMUNICATION

FORMAL NOTICE

ACKNOWLEDGEMENT OF OCCASION

BUREAU OF · COMMUNICATION
EST. 1860

STEP ONE
WRITE THE NAME
OF SENDER HERE

STEP TWO
NEATLY WRITE THE
NAME AND ADDRESS
OF RECIPIENT HERE

AFFIX
POSTAGE
IN THIS
SPACE

A Token of My Affections

To My Dearest ...., From Your ....
 NAME OF RECIPIENT   TITLE   NAME OF SENDER

How are You? It doesn't matter, for I am about to make your day!

In this .... day and age, we too rarely show appreciation
 [MODERN/SELFISH/DASTARDLY]

for each other. I've decided it's high time to do something about it, so

I'm giving you a .... Yes, it may be hard to
 EFFUSIVE ADJECTIVE   GIFT

believe, and you are surely saying, "Heavens no! That is far too

.... of you!" but let me assure you that it is deserved.
 [GENEROUS/INSIGHTFUL/BRILLIANT]

Please, treasure this gift! It is more than a reminder of me

and my generous affections. You should see it not just as a first-class

............................., but as a celebration of your ....
 KIND OF GIFT   UNIQUE SKILL OR CHARACTERISTIC

Lest you scheme up a way to repay me, let me say that no reciprocation

is called for. I may even go so far as to refuse your gift — That is how

serious I am. Unless of course you offer me ....
                                            A PARTICULARLY ALLURING THING

THE

FEDERAL BUREAU
OF
COMMUNICATION

EST. 1860

FORMAL NOTICE

A TOKEN OF MY AFFECTIONS

STEP ONE
WRITE THE NAME
OF SENDER HERE

STEP TWO
NEATLY WRITE THE
NAME AND ADDRESS
OF RECIPIENT HERE

AFFIX
POSTAGE
IN THIS
SPACE

NOTIFICATION OF WHEREABOUTS

POST CARD

GREETINGS FROM ....! I HAVE BEEN
LOCATION OF SENDER

HERE FOR ...., AND I SHOULD HAVE
PERIOD OF TIME

WRITTEN SOONER, BUT ....
INPLAUSIBLE EXCUSE

THE WEATHER IS ...., AND IT IS VERY
GENERAL DESCRIPTION OF CLIMATE

.... HERE. THE
UNIQUE PROPERTY OF SENDER'S LOCATION

LOCALS ARE QUITE ...., AND
DESCRIPTION OF INDIGENOUS PEOPLES

THE OTHER DAY I ATE A .... COVERED IN
FOOD OR INSECT

.... BASICALLY, I AM HAVING A
POWDER OR LIQUID

.... TIME, THOUGH I LOOK FORWARD TO
CANDID STATEMENT

.... WHEN/IF I RETURN.
THING MISSED FROM HOME

................, YOUR ...., ...
SENTIMENT   TITLE   NAME OF SENDER

FOR OFFICIAL USE ONLY

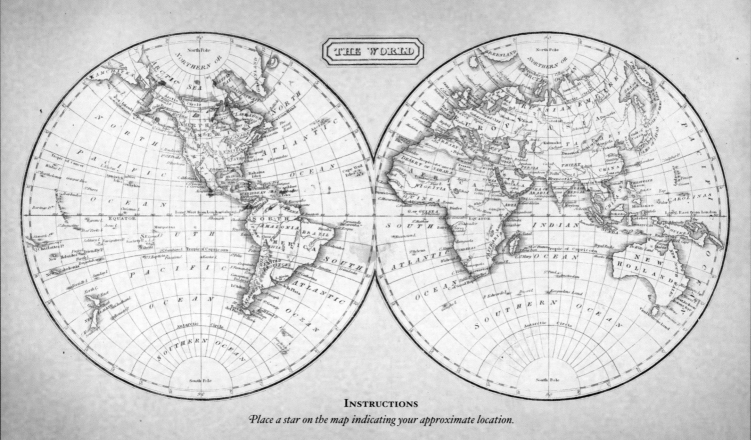

THE WORLD

INSTRUCTIONS

Place a star on the map indicating your approximate location.

RECOMMENDED INVESTMENT

UC-227

STATEMENT

DEAR ...., THE OTHER DAY I WAS
NAME OF RECIPIENT

PERUSING THE MERCHANDISE IN ....,
NAME OF STORE

WHEN I SAW A ....
DESCRIPTIVE ADJECTIVE   *NAME OF ITEM*

IT WAS SO ...., I FELT OBLIGATED TO TELL
ADJECTIVE

YOU. FRANKLY, I HAVE NEVER SEEN ANYTHING LIKE IT —

IT LOOKS LIKE A .... AND IS
OBJECT OF COMPARISON

.... ALL I CAN SAY IS:
EXTRAORDINARY PROPERTY OF ITEM

.................................! I FIRMLY BELIEVE THAT
EXCLAMATION OR PROCLAMATION

☐ YOU ☐ ME ☐ EVERYONE SHOULD GET ONE. IN FACT,

I WOULD GLADLY ....
EXTREME ACTION

TO HAVE ONE RIGHT NOW. YOU SHOULD REVIEW IT IMME-

DIATELY. I ANTICIPATE YOU WILL BE ....
REACTION

SINCERELY, YOUR ....
RELATION TO RECIPIENT   *NAME OF SENDER*

RATIONALITY OF INVESTMENT

INSANE — JUSTIFIABLE — TAX DEDUCTIBLE
◡ ◡ ◡ ◡ ◡ ◡ ◡

PROS

- ☐ SHEER SEX APPEAL
- ☐ LIMITED AVAILABILITY
- ☐ UTTER EXTRAVAGANCE
- ☐ INTIMIDATE NEIGHBORS
- ☐ SUPPORT ARTISANS
- ☐ TO CREATE ENVY
- ☐ IT IS ORANGE
- ....

CONS

- ☐ EXORBITANT COST
- ☐ CONSPICUOUS
- ☐ UNWEARABLE
- ☐ TOO BIG
- ☐ TOO SMALL
- ☐ LACK OF SPACE
- ☐ IT IS ORANGE
- ....

RECOMMENDATIONS

- ☐ I PLAN TO GET ONE
- ☐ YOU SHOULD GET ONE
- ☐ YOU SHOULD GIVE ME ONE

LIKELIHOOD OF REGRET

IMPOSSIBLE — WHEN THE BILL ARRIVES — IMMEDIATE
◡ ◡ ◡ ◡ ◡ ◡ ◡

ADDITIONAL NOTES

FOR THOSE WHO ARE LESS THAN SPEECHLESS

....

....

THE BUREAU OF · COMMUNICATION

FORMAL NOTICE

RECOMMENDED INVESTMENT

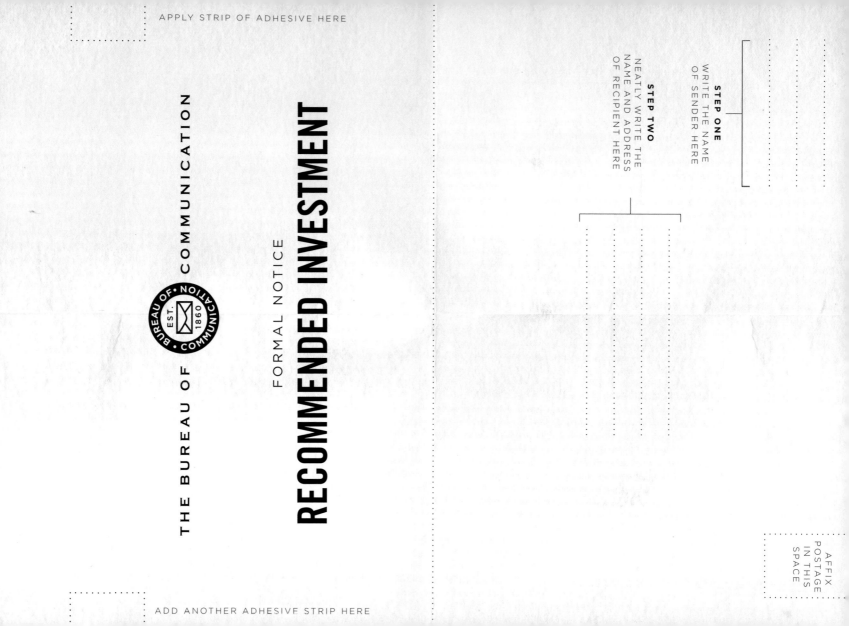

STEP ONE
WRITE THE NAME
OF SENDER HERE

STEP TWO
NEATLY WRITE THE
NAME AND ADDRESS
OF RECIPIENT HERE

AFFIX
POSTAGE
IN THIS
SPACE

BUREAU OF COMMUNICATION

MISTAKE REPORT

Recorded for posterity

FORM M-1292

CLASSIFICATION
- [ ] Personal
- [ ] Professional
- [ ] Existential

MISTAKE DESCRIPTION:

....

(I.E. Using a stolen credit card, Storing a pen in a shirt pocket, Skiing while intoxicated)

RELEVANT BACKGROUND INFORMATION

NAME OF PERSON FILING REPORT	OCCUPATION	AGE	LOCATION OF INCIDENT

NAME OF OTHER PERSON/S INVOLVED	OCCUPATION	RELATIONSHIP	TIME OF INCIDENT

INCIDENT DETAILS

EXPLAIN THE SITUATION:

....
....
....

WHAT YOU THOUGHT WOULD HAPPEN:

....
....

- [ ] *I knew that this was unlikely.*

WHAT ACTUALLY HAPPENED:

....
....

- [ ] *I was not surprised.*

CONCLUSIONS

LIST CONSEQUENCES/COSTS/DAMAGES:

....
....
....

- [ ] *Additional effects cannot be calculated.*

SUMMARIZE THE LESSON LEARNED FROM THIS EXPERIENCE:

"...
...."

- [ ] *I intend to follow this advice.*

LIKELIHOOD OF REPEATED OCCURRENCE *Select one:*

INEVITABLE — STATISTICALLY PROBABLE — GOD FORBID

○ ○ ○ ○ ○ ○

THIS MISTAKE WAS:
- [ ] Educational
- [ ] Easily avoidable
- [ ] Embarrassing
- [ ] Expensive
- [ ] Enjoyable

I AM:
- [ ] Ashamed
- [ ] Scarred
- [ ] Stronger
- [ ] Wiser
- [ ] Still confused

I declare, under penalty of perjury, that the information I entered on this document is true and correct to the best of my knowledge.

SIGNATURE/INITIALS	DATE OF FILING	TIME

DO NOT WRITE IN THIS SPACE

— THANK YOU FOR WRITING NEATLY AND CLEARLY —

THE BUREAU OF COMMUNICATION

FORMAL NOTICE

MISTAKE REPORT

STEP ONE
WRITE THE NAME
OF SENDER HERE

STEP TWO
NEATLY WRITE THE
NAME AND ADRESS
OF RECIPIENT HERE

AFFIX
POSTAGE
IN THIS
SPACE

REPAYMENT PLAN

=== MESSAGE ===

Dear ....,
NAME OF LENDER

It is with a heavy hand that I write to you with .... NEWS.
NEGATIVE ADJECTIVE

I am unable to return the .... THAT YOU SO
ESSENTIAL RESOURCE

.... loaned me. My plan was simple — I would merely
SHAMELESS FLATTERY

...., and be left with plenty of ....
DESCRIPTION OF UNSUCCESSFUL SCHEME   RESOURCE

to return your .... to you. Through no fault of my own,
RESOURCE + INTEREST

...., and I was forced to .... INSTEAD.
A TERRIBLE THING HAPPENED   ALTERNATE PLAN PURSUED

I assure you, I have every intention of repaying you, if not with the actual

...., then with ...., which I am sure you
BORROWED THING   ITEM OF EQUAL OR LESSER VALUE

agree is worth just as much.

I would be grateful if you would kindly reply with a promise that we will

be able to maintain our .... relationship. It would
AFFECTIONATE ADJECTIVE

.... me to think that my .... has somehow tarnished it.
NEGATIVE EFFECT   SELF DEPRECATION

Sincerely, your humbled friend, ...
YOUR NAME WRITTEN WITHOUT CAPITALIZATION

BUREAU OF COMMUNICATION EST. 1860

FORMAL NOTICE

REPAYMENT PLAN

THE BUREAU OF COMMUNICATION

STEP ONE
WRITE THE NAME
OF SENDER HERE

STEP TWO
NEATLY WRITE THE
NAME AND ADDRESS
OF RECIPIENT HERE

AFFIX
POSTAGE
IN THIS
SPACE

SALE NOTICE

FILING DATE

ATTENTION

Calling all Neighbors, Friends & Speculators!

I AM PLEASED TO ANNOUNCE THE SALE OF MY

.... IT IS
ADJECTIVE   ITEM

AN OUTSTANDING SPECIMEN OF A ....
ITEM CATEGORY

THAT HAS SERVED ME WELL BOTH AS A ....
PRIMARY USAGE

AND .... I EXPECT IT TO PROVIDE YOU
ADDITIONAL USAGE

WITH YEARS OF .... SERVICE. IT IS DEFINITELY
[OCCASIONAL/ONGOING/RELIABLE]

WORTH KEEPING: IN FACT, THE ONLY REASON THAT I AM

SELLING IT IS BECAUSE ....
PLAUSIBLE EXCUSE FOR SALE

AN ITEM OF THIS QUALITY COULD EASILY FETCH

.... FAIRLY, BUT I AM SELLING IT FOR THE
EXAGGERATED PRICE

.... PRICE OF $............................. THIS
SALESMAN'S ADJECTIVE   TELL IT LIKE IT IS

IS/IS NOT NEGOTIABLE, THOUGH I MIGHT CONSIDER
CHOOSE ONE

TRADING THE ITEM FOR A USED ....
DESIRABLE GOOD

WARRANTY

I can Assure you that:

☐ IT WAS LIKE THAT WHEN I BOUGHT IT.

☐ YOU WILL BARELY NOTICE THE SCRATCHES.

☐ THE ITEM IN QUESTION WAS NOT STOLEN.

☐ I AM NOT A CROOK.

CONDITION

PRISTINE — RUSTY — BROKEN
○ ○ ○ ○ ○ ○ ○

ILLUSTRATION

NOT TO SCALE

FRONT | SIDE

TOP | SUGGESTED USAGE

FINE PRINT

WHILE I CAN ASSURE YOU THAT THE STATEMENTS MADE IN THIS DOCUMENT HAVE NOT BEEN KNOWINGLY FALSIFIED, THE CLAIMS MADE WITHIN CANNOT BE BACKED UP. I HAVE NOT ACTUALLY USED THE ITEM FOR ITS INTENDED PURPOSE IN OVER FIVE YEARS. ALL SALES ARE ABSOLUTELY FINAL — I OFFER NO SATISFACTION GUARANTEE. CAVEAT EMPTOR!

BUREAU OF COMMUNICATION · EST. 1860

THE BUREAU OF · COMMUNICATION

FORMAL NOTICE

SALE NOTICE

STEP ONE
WRITE THE NAME
OF SENDER HERE

STEP TWO
NEATLY WRITE THE
NAME AND ADDRESS
OF RECIPIENT HERE

AFFIX
POSTAGE
IN THIS
SPACE

STATEMENT

DEAR ...., I CAN NO LONGER
NAME AND TITLE OF RECIPIENT

CONTAIN MYSELF. I NEED TO LET YOU KNOW THAT I FEEL

YOUR .... IS
ISSUE REQUIRING FEEDBACK

QUITE .... I WOULD PROPOSE THAT
YOUR FEELING ABOUT THE ISSUE

YOU CONSIDER ...., BECAUSE
PROPOSED SOLUTION

IF YOU DO NOT, ...
UNINTENDED, UNDESIRABLE CONSEQUENCE

ALL THIS MAY COME AS NEWS TO YOU, THOUGH I CAN

ASSURE YOU THAT IT HAS BEEN GOING ON SINCE

.... I WOULD HAVE INFORMED YOU
TIME WHEN ISSUE BEGAN

SOONER, THOUGH I ....
YOUR EXCUSE FOR SILENCE

IF YOU DO MANAGE TO MAKE THIS CHANGE, I GUARANTEE

.... SURELY, THIS WOULD
HYPERBOLE-LADEN PROMISE

BE PREFERABLE. THANK YOU FOR YOUR CONSIDERATION.

TRULY, ☐ ANONYMOUS. ☐ SIGNED, ...
NAME OF SENDER

WHO FEELS THIS WAY

ONLY ME — EVERYONE YOU KNOW — STRANGERS, TOO
○ ○ ○ ○ ○ ○ ○

WHY WE HAVE KEPT QUIET

☐ WE KNOW IT IS A SENSITIVE SUBJECT.

☐ WE THOUGHT YOU ALREADY KNEW.

☐ WE HOPED IT WOULD SOLVE ITSELF.

☐ WE EXPECTED SOMEONE ELSE TO MENTION IT.

WHY WE CHOSE TO SPEAK UP

☐ YOU ARE OTHERWISE A GOOD PERSON.

☐ YOUR OFFENSE IS A BURDEN ON OTHERS.

☐ THIS CHANGE WOULD IMPROVE OUR LIVES.

☐ ALL ATTEMPTS AT SUBTLETY HAVE FAILED.

WE IMPLORE YOU:

☐ SEEK HELP.

☐ DO NOT TAKE THIS PERSONALLY.

☐ DO NOT IGNORE THIS MESSAGE.

☐ KEEP US ALERTED OF OUR FLAWS.

☐ LET US NEVER SPEAK OF THIS AGAIN.

FURTHER INSIGHT
HONESTY IS A VIRTUE

....

....

THE BUREAU OF COMMUNICATION

BUREAU OF · COMMUNICATION · EST. 1860

FORMAL NOTICE

UNSOLICITED FEEDBACK

STEP ONE
WRITE THE NAME
OF SENDER HERE

STEP TWO
NEATLY WRITE THE
NAME AND ADDRESS
OF RECIPIENT HERE

AFFIX
POSTAGE
IN THIS
SPACE

PASSIVE-AGRESSIVE REMINDER

FORM **11-22**

BUREAU OF COMMUNICATION · EST. 1860

FILING DATE

MESSAGE

DEAR ....,
NAME OF RECIPIENT

I HAVE RECENTLY EXPERIENCED A MOST ....
UNPLEASANT FEELING

EVENT. I DISTINCTLY RECALL YOU AND I DISCUSSING A

☐ PLAN   ☐ PROMISE   ☐ GUARANTEE   ☐ SCHEME   TO

....,
DESCRIPTION OF WHAT YOU REMEMBER DISCUSSING

THOUGH I DO NOT BELIEVE THAT SUCH A THING HAS

COME TO PASS. I CANNOT HELP BUT WONDER IF I AM

EXPERIENCING ☐ HALLUCINATIONS ☐ WAKING DREAMS

☐ REVERSE AMNESIA. I FEAR FOR THE WORST. SO PLEASE,

DO TELL ME IF YOU ALSO RECALL THE DISCUSSION SO

THAT I CAN LEARN WHETHER OR NOT I AM CRAZY. AND IF

THE CONVERSATION DID INDEED TAKE PLACE, PLEASE DO

PROCEED WITH THE PLAN AS I REMEMBER IT OCCURRING.

AS ALWAYS, I APPRECIATE YOUR VIRTUOUS HONESTY.

THANK YOU, YOUR ...., ...
RELATIONSHIP TO RECIPIENT   NAME OF SENDER

LET US TURN TO LOGIC

REGARDING MY MEMORY OF THIS PLAN, I SEE ONLY THREE POSSIBILITIES:

I Am Wrong:

☐ PERHAPS I HAVE SENT THIS LETTER TO THE WRONG PERSON? IF SO, I BEG YOUR FORGIVENESS FOR ANY UNDUE STRESS.

☐ EARLIER IN THIS LETTER I WAS JUST BEING SARCASTIC, BUT IT *IS* POSSIBLE THAT I SIMPLY IMAGINED THE EVENT.

You Are Wrong:

☐ I AM SURE YOU HAVE A SEMI-PLAUSIBLE EXCUSE FOR YOUR SHORTCOMING.

☐ NO DOUBT THE SITUATION WILL BE RECTIFIED IN AN EXPEDIENT FASHION.

☐ YOU WILL GENEROUSLY SHOULDER ANY FINANCIAL CONSEQUENCES DUE TO YOUR FAILURE TO ACCOMPLISH THE PLAN.

We Are Both Wrong:

☐ PERHAPS THE TASK HAS ALREADY BEEN COMPLETED BUT YOU FAILED TO ADEQUATELY NOTIFY ME?

☐ PERHAPS WE MISCOMMUNICATED AND YOU BELIEVE THAT YOU HAVE NOT MADE AN ERROR.

☐ HOW COULD BOTH OF US BE WRONG? IT SEEMS QUITE IMPROBABLE.

THE BUREAU OF · COMMUNICATION

FORMAL NOTICE

PASSIVE-AGGRESSIVE REMINDER

BUREAU OF · COMMUNICATION
EST. 1860

STEP ONE
WRITE THE NAME
OF SENDER HERE

STEP TWO
NEATLY WRITE THE
NAME AND ADDRESS
OF RECIPIENT HERE

AFFIX
POSTAGE
IN THIS
SPACE

Ignore This Notice at Your Peril

Having repeatedly warned you of the consequences of _____

Having suffered the pain of your _____

Having exhausted every reasonable measure in dealing with you.

Having been thwarted in all my attempts to live and let live.

Having accepted that you are an annoying _____

Having been insulted by your _____ and _____

Having put up with _____

and Having seen no change in your behavior:

It is Clear that the Time for Diplomacy has Ended.

THEREFORE, THROUGH THIS OFFICIAL NOTICE

I FORMALLY DECLARE WAR

Although it is true that my warmongering may be constrained by my natural and ample wells of compassion and moderation, a deeply rooted habit of chivalrous conduct, and a persnickety obedience to the minute strictures of international law, Let it be publicly and privately known that despite my compunctions, I still intend to embark vigorously, without delay, and with single minded focus to:

Grind your _____ into _____ and

Smash your _____ against _____ and

Wipe that _____ off your face forever.

Without your timely capitulation I will have no choice but to lay waste to your business and personal affairs, to confound all your enterprises and relationships, and to take great enjoyment in destroying and despoiling the things you love the most.

For your sake, therefore, I advise you to render your complete and abject submission to me, including pathetic and profuse pleas for mercy, and begging me to slake my righteous anger. Additionally, you would be well advised to make a peace offering of _____ and to perform _____ before I can express the full measure of my wrath.

Otherwise, Face Destruction, in every sense of the phrase.

Thank you for your prompt surrender.

PLEASE REFER TO THE VARIOUS GENEVA CONVENTIONS RE: LEGALLY PERMISSIBLE AND ALLOWED MAYHEM AND DESTRUCTION.

DECLARATION OF WAR

FORMAL NOTICE

THE
BUREAU
OF
COMMUNICATION

STEP ONE
WRITE THE NAME
OF SENDER HERE

STEP TWO
NEATLY WRITE THE
NAME AND ADRESS
OF RECIPIENT HERE

AFFIX
POSTAGE
IN THIS
SPACE

Wartime Services

Between the years of 1870-1940, the Bureau continued to explore its curious niche, creating forms primarily in the realm of interpersonal communication. From time to time, it was called upon to provide design services to other branches of the government, such as the IRS and War Department.

Soon it would find a new mission: With the start of World War II, America found itself stretched thinner than ever before and faced shortages both of consumer goods and manpower. As the FBI rapidly increased the size of its intelligence staff from the ranks of white collar workers, it became difficult for civilians to find legal aid for even the simplest of tasks.

At the personal request of President Roosevelt, the Bureau took it upon itself to alleviate the demand for lawyers, drafting a set of templates more precisely worded than any that had come before. Among these were three of the most common legal forms: The Universal Contract, the Non-Disclosure Agreement, and the Termination Letter.

While little research was done as to the effectiveness of the new forms, it is clear that America pulled itself through the drought of paper-pushers, no doubt thanks to the Bureau of Communication. After the war, as the U.S. returned to a period of prosperity, the habit of using standardized legal templates fell out of vogue as expensive lawyers were once again able to create fully customized contracts – though the template forms continued to be used by some of the thriftier portions of the populace.

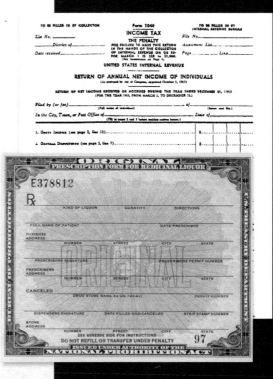

The Bureau was responsible for designing a variety of government documents, most famously the first 1040 Income tax return, along with prescriptions for medicinal alcohol used during the Prohibition.

Cutbacks and Closure

By the 1960s, the Bureau's existence could be attributed more to governmental negligence than cultural relevance. Cutbacks affected all branches of the government as the space program monopolized spending, and the Bureau was able to keep its doors open thanks only to a surplus of two-dollar bills created by the Bureau of Engraving and Printing. After 1964, the Bureau paid for all its printing, ink, and miscellaneous expenses in cash.

Despite attempting to maintain a low profile, the Bureau still continued to develop new forms, including a series of "Universal" forms designed for romantic purposes – though they failed to gain widespread acceptance.

Not all hope was lost – the rise of so-called "free love" movement led to an increase in the popularity of some of the classic forms, particularly the Formal Apology and Statement of Regret; while the chivalrous tone of the Marriage Proposal was deemed anachronistic and the form was taken out of print. It remains one of the rarest forms in the collection.

The long history of the Bureau came to an unceremonious end in 1973 at the hand of President Richard Nixon, who spent many years campaigning against the spread of communist ideology. The President received a Formal Apology from an aide, but with his notoriously bad eyesight, he misread the logo as saying "The Bureau of Communism". Even after correction, he remained wary, calling the forms "non-humorous and un-American." Soon all the documents and archives of the B.o.C. office were seized and the twelve employees lost their jobs. Not a single newspaper carried the story.

The entire archive of the B.o.C. remained in storage until 2007, when your authors used the Freedom of Information Act to requisition the documents. Since then, we have carefully restored each form, and have even begun the process of developing new series of Formal Notices in order to preserve this essential piece of American History.

FORMAL INTRODUCTION

═══ REPLETE WITH SOCIAL NICETIES ═══

BUREAU OF · COMMUNIC·ATION
EST. 1860

To ☐ My friend ☐ My dearest ☐ The venerable ....,

I wish to present to you my ...., a .... by trade, a person whose pleasant .... and irreproachable .... have embold-ened me to bring the two of you together. I have mentioned your name as my most cherished .... Like you, ... is ...., which leads me to believe that you will find a great deal in common.

At a minimum, you share a mutual friend in myself, and if conversation grows dry, you are welcome to discuss the matter of my .... If that proves fruitless, there's always everyone's favorite topic: .... In the worst case, you can always fall back on a banal conversation about the weather. Or, even if friendship fails to develop, your professional pursuits may be aligned, and and you might wish to consider employing him.

Understand that any care shown to him will be regarded as a personal favor to myself. That said, I beg a thousand apologies if my friend in some way reflects poorly on me. Off the record, he can be a bit of a .... In time, you will surely learn to overlook this shortcoming, and one day, you may not even notice it.

Eternally indebted to you,

....

Postscript — Entirely aside from the matter at hand, I send my highest regards and most respectful compliments. And send my regards to .... for me.

FORMAL INTRODUCTION LETTER, PREPARED BY THE B.O.C. WASHINGTON DC

THE BUREAU OF COMMUNICATION

OFFICIAL NOTICE

FORMAL INTRODUCTION

STEP ONE
WRITE THE NAME
OF SENDER HERE

STEP TWO
NEATLY WRITE THE
NAME AND ADDRESS
OF RECIPIENT HERE

AFFIX
POSTAGE
IN THIS
SPACE

PERSONAL DOCUMENTATION
UNIVERSAL COVER LETTER
FORM NX-11

APPLYING FOR POSITIONS: ☐ PROFESSIONAL ☐ ROMANTIC ☐ BOTH

Dear Sir/Madam:

I am informed that you seek a .... As a ...., I am quite interested in this ....
  ROLE   KIND OF PERSON   ADJECTIVE
opportunity. I have held a position in the past with .... , who I am certain will vouch for my ....
                                                      PREVIOUS EMPLOYER/LOVER   APPLICABLE SKILL
I currently spend my time by ...., and I find myself with a desire to upgrade to this new role because
                              TIME CONSUMING ACTIVITY
.... In exchange for my .... services, I ask for only .... and
MOTIVATION FOR CHANGE   SKILLS OFFERED   COMPENSATION
.... This may sound like very little, but you must understand how excited I am to .... with you.
ADDITIONAL FAVORS   VERB
Please contact me at once, for I have already entertained offers from ...., and it would truly be a pity for you
                                                                        COMPETING BUSINESSES/LOVERS
to lose such a .... candidate as myself. Thank you for your time, and I look forward to hearing from you. ....
              FLATTERING ADJECTIVE   SENDER'S NAME

DEAR RECIPIENT: BELOW YOU WILL FIND TWO CONVENIENT RECEIPT FORMS. PLEASE CUT OUT AND COMPLETE THE APPROPRIATE FORM AND RETURN TO SENDER.

COVER LETTER RECEIPT
POSITIVE RESPONSE

Dear Mr./Mrs./Ms. ....,
                    APPLICANT'S NAME
Thank you for sending that lovely form letter. While I cannot
attest to your eligibility, I appreciate your .... and
                                              VIRTUE
would be pleased to meet with you as soon as possible. You
would be well-advised to bring .... and a
                                RELEVANT ITEMS
.... I look forward to assessing our compatibility.
USEFUL OBJECT
                              Sincerely, ...
                                        SENDER'S NAME

COVER LETTER RECEIPT
NEGATIVE RESPONSE

Dear Mr./Mrs./Ms. ....,
                    APPLICANT'S NAME
Regrettably, we have received many applications to the open
position, and though we have not yet selected a candidate, it is
clear that you are too .... for the role. Thus, we
                       CRUEL ADJECTIVE
should both save our precious time and pursue more probable
endeavors. Good luck with whatever it is that you wind up doing.

                              Seriously, ...
                                        SENDER'S NAME

APPLY STRIP OF ADHESIVE HERE

THE BUREAU OF COMMUNICATION

FORMAL NOTICE

UNIVERSAL COVER LETTER

STEP ONE
WRITE THE NAME
OF SENDER HERE

STEP TWO
NEATLY WRITE THE
NAME AND ADDRESS
OF RECIPIENT HERE

AFFIX
POSTAGE
IN THIS
SPACE

ADD ANOTHER ADHESIVE STRIP HERE

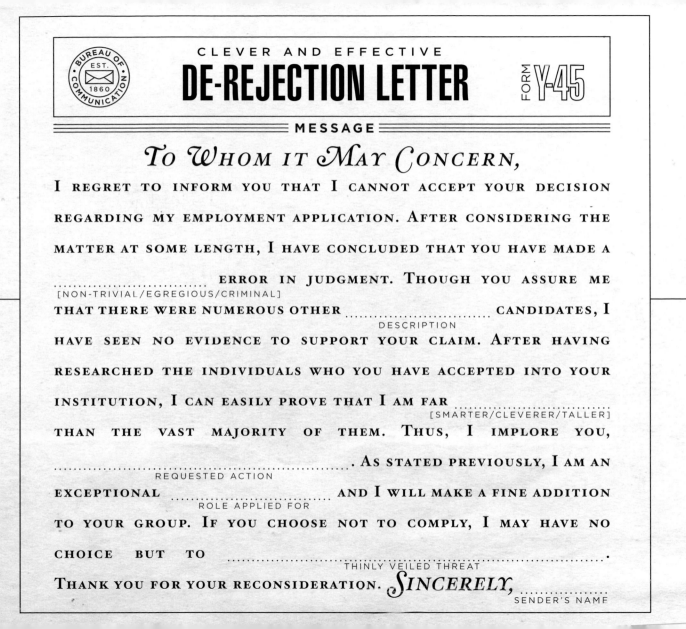

CLEVER AND EFFECTIVE
DE-REJECTION LETTER
FORM Y-45

BUREAU OF COMMUNICATION · EST. 1860

═══ MESSAGE ═══

To Whom it May Concern,

I REGRET TO INFORM YOU THAT I CANNOT ACCEPT YOUR DECISION REGARDING MY EMPLOYMENT APPLICATION. AFTER CONSIDERING THE MATTER AT SOME LENGTH, I HAVE CONCLUDED THAT YOU HAVE MADE A .... ERROR IN JUDGMENT. THOUGH YOU ASSURE ME
[NON-TRIVIAL/EGREGIOUS/CRIMINAL]
THAT THERE WERE NUMEROUS OTHER .... CANDIDATES, I
DESCRIPTION
HAVE SEEN NO EVIDENCE TO SUPPORT YOUR CLAIM. AFTER HAVING RESEARCHED THE INDIVIDUALS WHO YOU HAVE ACCEPTED INTO YOUR INSTITUTION, I CAN EASILY PROVE THAT I AM FAR ....
[SMARTER/CLEVERER/TALLER]
THAN THE VAST MAJORITY OF THEM. THUS, I IMPLORE YOU, ... AS STATED PREVIOUSLY, I AM AN
REQUESTED ACTION
EXCEPTIONAL .... AND I WILL MAKE A FINE ADDITION
ROLE APPLIED FOR
TO YOUR GROUP. IF YOU CHOOSE NOT TO COMPLY, I MAY HAVE NO CHOICE BUT TO ....
THINLY VEILED THREAT
THANK YOU FOR YOUR RECONSIDERATION. *Sincerely*, ...
SENDER'S NAME

FORMAL NOTICE

DE-REJECTION LETTER

THE BUREAU OF COMMUNICATION

STEP ONE
WRITE THE NAME
OF SENDER HERE

STEP TWO
NEATLY WRITE THE
NAME AND ADDRESS
OF RECIPIENT HERE

AFFIX
POSTAGE
IN THIS
SPACE

THE BUREAU OF COMMUNICATION

UNIVERSAL

NON-DISCLOSURE AGREEMENT

This is an agreement between .... (Hereafter referred to as "We") and
NAME OF SECRET HOLDER

.... (referred to as "You") regarding the subject of .... ("The Secret").
NAME OF IGNORANT PARTY   CONFIDENTIAL INFORMATION

By signing this document, You agree to these terms both retroactively and in perpetuity:

1. MAINTAINING THE SECRECY OF THE SECRET IS OF THE UTMOST IMPORTANCE. UNDER NO CIRCUMSTANCES SHOULD You DISCLOSE ITS NATURE TO LOVERS, FRIENDS, FAMILY MEMBERS, PRIESTS, SPIRITUAL ADVISORS, OR ANY EMPLOYEE OF A GOVERNMENTAL AGENCY. IF THE SECRET COMES UP SOCIALLY, YOU ARE INSTRUCTED TO BEGIN SNEEZING VIOLENTLY UNTIL THE INQUIRY SUBSIDES. IF SUBPOENAED, You ARE INSTRUCTED TO PLEAD IGNORANCE AND MAKE A REFERENCE TO A FAMILIAL HISTORY OF ALZHEIMER'S DISEASE.

2. THE SECRET'S CODE NAME MUST NEVER BE SPOKEN ALOUD. THE SECRET ITSELF MUST NOT BE WRITTEN ON PAPER. YOU WILL BE EXPECTED TO MEMORIZE ANY PERTINENT INFORMATION — MNEMONIC DEVICES OR MEMORY ENHANCING DRUGS ARE NOT PERMITTED.

3. WHENEVER We ALLOW You TO MEET WITH US, You SHOULD ENTER THE PREMISES VIA THE REAR DOOR MARKED "LOADING DOCK." IF We DEEM IT NECESSARY, You CONSENT TO BE BLINDFOLDED AND TO WEAR EARMUFFS WHILE BEING ESCORTED THROUGH THE PREMISES.

4. THE SECRET MAY ONLY BE DISCUSSED WITHIN A COLD, WINDOWLESS ROOM. ALL CORRESPON- DENCE SHOULD BE WRITTEN WITH INVISIBLE INK. MAIL ROOM STAFF AND POSTAL EMPLOYEES CANNOT BE TRUSTED WITH THE SECRET, THUS DOCUMENTS CAN ONLY BE EXCHANGED BY SLIPPING THEM UNDER THE LOCKED DOOR MARKED "PRIVATE."

5. WE RESERVE THE RIGHT TO MONITOR BOTH PERSONAL AND PROFESSIONAL TELEPHONE CALLS AND WRITTEN CORRESPONDENCE. MANY OF OUR ASSOCIATES CHOOSE TO REFRAIN FROM ROMANTIC ENTANGLEMENTS OR TO DIVORCE FROM A EXISTING MARRIAGES. WHILE We CANNOT LEGALLY REQUIRE SUCH LIFESTYLE CHOICES, You ARE ENCOURAGED TO USE YOUR BEST JUDGMENT.

6. IN ALL FUTURE COMMUNICATIONS, You WILL IDENTIFY YOURSELF BY YOUR CODE NAME (WRITTEN BELOW). We WILL REFER TO You ONLY BY YOUR NINE-DIGIT SOCIAL SECURITY NUMBER.

7. THE TERMS AND LANGUAGE OF THIS AGREEMENT ARE ALSO CONFIDENTIAL.

IF You ARE FOUND TO HAVE OR SUSPECTED OF BREACHING THE TERMS OF THIS AGREEMENT, WE WILL TERMINATE OUR RELATIONSHIP WITH EXTREME PREJUDICE. We WILL DISAVOW ANY KNOW- LEDGE OF You. We WILL ALSO WITHHOLD ANY MONIES DUE, AND MAY CONFISCATE VALUABLE PERSONAL POSSESSIONS. You MAY ALSO BE HELD ACCOUNTABLE IN A COURT OF LAW FOR DAMAGES BOTH FINANCIAL AND EMOTIONAL ARISING EVEN INDIRECTLY FROM YOUR TRESPASS.

"I agree to be bound by these reasonable precautions to protect the confidentiality of the aforemen- tioned Secret, and understand that my strict observance to these procedures is required to continue the relationship. I voluntarily sign away my rights and freedoms for the privilege of learning the Secret."

....
YOUR SIGNATURE   SOCIAL SECURITY NUMBER   CODE NAME OF AGENT

Any three men can share a secret if two of them are dead.
BENJAMIN FRANKLIN

APPLY STRIP OF ADHESIVE HERE

ADD ANOTHER ADHESIVE STRIP HERE

THE
BUREAU
OF
COMMUNICATION

FORMAL NOTICE

NON-DISCLOSURE AGREEMENT

STEP ONE
WRITE THE NAME
OF SENDER HERE

STEP TWO
NEATLY WRITE THE
NAME AND ADDRESS
OF RECIPIENT HERE

AFFIX
POSTAGE
IN THIS
SPACE

THE BUREAU OF COMMUNICATION

UNIVERSAL CONTRACT

A FORM FOR MEN OF SOUND MIND, ABLE BODY, AND UTMOST INTEGRITY, FAR SMARTER THAN THE MAJORITY OF THEIR BRETHREN. DO NOT SQUANDER YOUR HARD-EARNED MONIES BY COMMISSIONING LEGAL AIDE TO FORMULATE A SIMPLE CONTRACT. FILL OUT THIS FORM, SIGN IT, AND FOREVER BE BOUND BY YOUR AGREEMENT.

THE TERMS

I, ... (*REFERRED TO AS "PARTY A"*) *HEREBY AGREE TO*
   NAME OF FIRST PARTY

.... *TO/FOR* ....
                          NAME OF SECOND PARTY

("PARTY B") IN EXCHANGE FOR .... , *DUE* ....
                              A FEE, OBJECT, OR SERVICE   DATE OR TIME

ACTION OR SERVICE TO BE RENDERED

AGREEMENTS

WE HEREBY VOW: *To* COMPLETE THE TERMS OF THIS CONTRACT IN A TIMELY FASHION. *To* FULFILL OUR OBLIGATIONS TO THE UTMOST OF OUR ABILITIES. *To* PROCEED WITH DIGNITY, HONOR, AND FIDELITY. *To* CONSIDER THE OTHER PARTY'S INTERESTS EQUAL TO OUR OWN. *To* PROMOTE CLEAR AND TRANSPARENT COMMUNICATION.

DAMAGES

IF EITHER PARTY FAILS TO FULFILL HIS CONTRACTUAL OBLIGATIONS, THIS CONTRACT ENTERS A STATE OF BREACH AND THE OTHER PARTY IS NO LONGER OBLIGATED TO UPHOLD HIS END OF THE AGREEMENT. AS AN INCENTIVE TO UPHOLD THE CONTRACT, BOTH PARTIES OFFER FORTH THE FOLLOWING ITEMS AS COLLATERAL:

....
A NON-TRIVIAL SUM   A HUMILIATING SECRET

....
A CHERISHED POSSESSION

PARTY A COLLATERAL

....
A NON-TRIVIAL SUM   A HUMILIATING SECRET

....
A CHERISHED POSSESSION

PARTY B COLLATERAL

CONFLICT RESOLUTION

AS A GESTURE OF GOOD FAITH, THE PARTY WHO BREACHES THE CONTRACT AGREES TO TRANSFER OWNERSHIP OF THE *CHERISHED POSSESSION* TO THE OTHER PARTY, PAY CASH DAMAGES EQUAL TO A *NON-TRIVIAL SUM*, AND TO PUBLICLY DECLARE THEIR *HUMILIATING SECRET*, ALONGSIDE A PHOTOGRAPHIC SELF-PORTRAIT, VIA AN ADVERTISEMENT IN A MAJOR METROPOLITAN NEWSPAPER.

AS THIS IS A CONTRACT FORMULATED WITHOUT THE ASSISTANCE OF A LAWYER, COURTS, OR A DICTIONARY, THERE IS NO NEED TO BECOME EMBROILED WITHIN THE SOCIAL SYSTEM BY ATTEMPTING TO RESOLVE A DISPUTE IN FRONT OF A JUDGE. MOREOVER, MANY OF THE TRADITIONAL TECHNIQUES OF CONFLICT RESOLUTION, INCLUDING ANIMOSITY, SUBTERFUGE, AND REVENGE, ARE ALL SLOW AND IMPRACTICAL. IN THE EVENT OF A DISAGREEMENT, BOTH PARTIES MUST ATTEMPT ARBITRATION BY A NEUTRAL PARTY OF EQUAL STATURE, TO BE MUTUALLY AGREED UPON. WHEN ARBITRATION FAILS, A PUBLIC DUEL HELD IN ACCORDANCE OF THE LAWS OF THE LAND SHOULD BE SUFFICIENT TO RESOLVE ANY OUTSTANDING GRIEVANCES.

IN CLOSING

WE ARE PLEASED THAT SUCH A FAIR AGREEMENT COULD BE REACHED, AND WE LOOK FORWARD TO FURTHERING EACH OTHER'S GOALS. WE HOPE FOR A SATISFACTORY RESOLUTION, BUT WILL SETTLE FOR A HUMILIATING ONE.

....
SIGNATURE OF PARTY A   SIGNATURE OF PARTY B

....
SIGNATURE OF PARTY A   DATE OF SIGNING

THE
BUREAU
OF
COMMUNICATION

FORMAL NOTICE

UNIVERSAL CONTRACT

STEP ONE
WRITE THE NAME
OF SENDER HERE

STEP TWO
NEATLY WRITE THE
NAME AND ADDRESS
OF RECIPIENT HERE

AFFIX
POSTAGE
IN THIS
SPACE

To the Honourable

....

RECIPIENT'S NAME, INCLUDING HONORARY TITLES

FOR YEARS WE'VE KNOWN YOU WERE *Good.* SOME OF US HAVE EVEN GONE SO FAR AS TO SAY *Great.* BUT NOW, WE CAN FINALLY GO AND CALL YOU *The Best.* THIS DOCUMENT SERVES AS FINAL AND INCONTROVERTIBLE PROOF OF YOUR ACHIEVEMENT AS A ....•

RECIPIENT'S OCCUPATION OR FIELD OF ACHIEVEMENT

Henceforth, You Shall be Referred to as a

BONA FIDE **Genius** CERTIFIED

NOW THAT YOUR BRILLIANCE HAS BEEN PROPERLY RECOGNIZED, PERHAPS IT IS TIME TO STEP ASIDE AND LET SOMEONE ELSE TRY THEIR HAND AT ....•....... THERE IS

OUTSTANDING SKILL

A WHOLE WORLD OF OTHER THINGS YOU COULD MASTER. FOR EXAMPLE, YOU MIGHT BE GOOD AT ....•.......

AN AMBITIOUS HOBBY

LEST YOUR HEAD SWELL TO TOO GREAT A PROPORTION, REMEMBER THAT BY YOUR AGE, ... HAD

FAMOUS HISTORICAL FIGURE

ALREADY ....•. IF YOU REALLY WANT TO LEAVE

NOTABLE ACHIEVEMENT

YOUR MARK, YOU WILL HAVE TO STOP ....AND GET

TIME WASTING HABIT

DOWN TO THE HARD WORK OF ....•......

TRUE VOCATION

CONGRATULATIONS, NOW, ONWARD AND UPWARD!

Presented by

....

NAME OF PRESENTERS

.... ON ....

DATE OF PRESENTATION

FORMAL NOTICE

CERTIFICATE OF GENIUS

THE BUREAU OF COMMUNICATION

STEP ONE
WRITE THE NAME
OF SENDER HERE

STEP TWO
NEATLY WRITE THE
NAME AND ADDRESS
OF RECIPIENT HERE

AFFIX
POSTAGE
IN THIS
SPACE

BUREAU OF COMMUNICATION
RECORD OF DISPUTE

SUBJECT OF DISPUTE

I.E. Proper storage of toothpaste, usage of paper towels, strange smells)

RELATIONSHIP
- ☐ Personal
- ☐ Professional
- ☐ Nonexistent

BIOGRAPHICAL FACTS

NAME OF AGGRESSOR	OCCUPATION	AGE	LOCATION OF INCIDENT
NAME OF DEFENDANT	OCCUPATION	AGE	DATE OF INCIDENT

INCIDENT DETAILS

DESCRIBE THE HISTORY OF THE SITUATION AND HOW THE DISPUTE BEGAN

SUMMARY OF AGGRESSOR'S CASE

SUMMARY OF DEFENDANT'S CASE

MEMORABLE QUOTE FROM AGGRESSOR

MEMORABLE QUOTE FROM DEFENDANT

ACTIONS TAKEN

Aggressor's Total Score ☐ | Points

☐ Shouting	-3 PTS	☐ Apologized	+3 PTS
☐ Swearing	-4 PTS	☐ Cried	+4 PTS
☐ Threats	-6 PTS	☐ Admitted guilt	+3 PTS
☐ Biting	-10 PTS	☐ Begged forgiveness	+10 PTS

Defendant's Total Score ☐ | Points

☐ Raised voice	-3 PTS	☐ Apologized	+3 PTS
☐ Defensive tone	-4 PTS	☐ Tears	+4 PTS
☐ Sarcasm	-6 PTS	☐ Admitted error	+3 PTS
☐ Theatrics	-10 PTS	☐ Gave forgiveness	+10 PTS

CONCLUSIONS

DESCRIBE HOW THE DISPUTE ENDED
Please remain as factual as possible. Subjective statements are unsuitable for public records.

A PLAN FOR HOW TO DEAL WITH THIS SITUATION IN THE FUTURE
Both parties should confer in an attempt to prevent future disputes.

SIGNATURE/INITIALS	DATE OF FILING	TIME	DESCRIBE THIS DISPUTE IN TWO WORDS

In the future, you will look back upon this fight and laugh – if you haven't killed each other first.

THE BUREAU OF COMMUNICATION

FORMAL NOTICE

RECORD OF DISPUTE

STEP ONE

WRITE THE NAME
OF SENDER HERE

STEP TWO

NEATLY WRITE THE
NAME AND ADDRESS
OF RECIPIENT HERE

AFFIX
POSTAGE
IN THIS
SPACE

FORM # 12-22B

UNIVERSAL
ABSENCE NOTE

PROPER AUTHORIZATION REQUIRED

CHECK ALL THAT APPLY

Dear _____
NAME OF RECIPIENT

Please excuse my absence from:

- ☐ Work
- ☐ School
- ☐ My Appointment
- ☐ Our Wedding
- ☐ _____

Please know that I wished above all to attend, but was foiled by:

- ☐ Sudden illness
- ☐ A misunderstanding with the law
- ☐ Temporary amnesia
- ☐ Saving the world
- ☐ An unexpected visitor
- ☐ _____

While I cannot reverse what I have done, to help rectify the situation:

- ☐ Please reschedule for _____
- ☐ I have attached a gift of _____
- ☐ Feel free to verbally berate me.

For more details, do not hesitate to contact:

- ☐ My Parents
- ☐ My Doctor
- ☐ My Spouse
- ☐ My Attorney
- ☐ The Chief of Police

_____
NAME OF SENDER

_____
SIGNATURE OF WITNESS/CORROBORATOR

BUREAU OF COMMUNICATION · EST. 1860

PRINTED BY THE BUREAU OF COMMUNICATION, WASHINGTON D.C. USA

APPLY STRIP OF ADHESIVE HERE

THE BUREAU OF COMMUNICATION

BUREAU OF · COMMUNICATION
EST. 1860

FORMAL NOTICE

ABSENCE NOTE

STEP ONE
WRITE THE NAME
OF SENDER HERE

STEP TWO
NEATLY WRITE THE
NAME AND ADDRESS
OF RECIPIENT HERE

AFFIX
POSTAGE
IN THIS
SPACE

ADD ANOTHER ADHESIVE STRIP HERE

UNIVERSAL
CEASE AND DESIST
TEMPLATE

Dear ....,

It has come to our attention that you have been
...., in direct
breach of both the law and the rules of common decency.

We have little choice but to insist that you immediately
.... and confirm
in writing that you will not repeat this infringement,
along with an effusive written apology.

A failure to comply with this request will be taken as a
sign of shameless arrogance and aggression. Do you know who
you are dealing with here? We hire only the most expensive
lawyers, who will surely seek compensation for damages that
have occurred and that someday may occur. Best of all, you
will be held responsible for their legal fees. All this
because of your .... conduct.

The situation begs the question: What, precisely, are
you thinking? That you are somehow above the law? Or that
perhaps we might overlook your little transgression? You
are wrong on both counts, my friend. We see everything. And
we wield the law like a .... that is used for
.... That is not a metaphor.

In case we have not been sufficiently clear, this will
be our final notice regarding the matter. We anticipate a
.... conclusion. Alternatively, we will
see you in court, and then prison.

Warm regards,

....

U.S. D.O.J STANDARD LEGAL FORMULAS, PREPARED BY THE B.O.C. WASHINGTON DC

APPLY STRIP OF ADHESIVE HERE

ADD ANOTHER ADHESIVE STRIP HERE

THE BUREAU OF COMMUNICATION

FORMAL NOTICE

CEASE AND DESIST

BUREAU OF · COMMUNICATION · EST. 1860

STEP ONE
WRITE THE NAME
OF SENDER HERE

STEP TWO
NEATLY WRITE THE
NAME AND ADDRESS
OF RECIPIENT HERE

AFFIX
POSTAGE
IN THIS
SPACE

UNIVERSAL
EMPLOYMENT
TERMINATION
FORMULA

Dear .... ,

Effective .... , your services at .... will no longer be required and your employ will be terminated.

Due to budgetary cutbacks and for our convenience, we have used this standardized termination template. Only the statements preceded by check marks apply to you.

☐ We regret to inform you of this news.

Your termination is due to:

☐ Your repeated ....
☐ Budgetary cutbacks from ....
☐ Interpersonal differences between ....
☐ Your tendency to ....
☐ Reasons which we cannot commit to writing.

After reviewing your file, we have concluded:

☐ There are some clear fabrications in your resume.
☐ We are unsure why you were ever even hired.
☐ It is remarkable that you lasted as long as you did.
☐ You should have pursued your dream of being a musician.

In summary:

☐ Your service was truly ....
☐ Advice for the future: ....
☐ We wish you good luck with your future endeavors.
☐ You would be ill-advised to request a recommendation.
☐ We have taken the liberty of emptying your desk.

Thank you for working at the aforementioned corporation.

Signed,

The Management

THE BUREAU OF COMMUNICATION

BUREAU OF COMMUNICATION · EST. 1860

FORMAL NOTICE

TERMINATION LETTER

STEP ONE
WRITE THE NAME
OF SENDER HERE

STEP TWO
NEATLY WRITE THE
NAME AND ADDRESS
OF RECIPIENT HERE

AFFIX
POSTAGE
IN THIS
SPACE

FILL - IN - THE - BLANK CORRESPONDENCE

RECORD OF INCORRECTNESS

I HOPE YOU'RE SITTING DOWN.

I AM GOING TO SAY SOMETHING MOMENTOUS. DO YOU RECALL WHEN

.... ?

IT TURNS OUT THAT I MAY HAVE MISCALCULATED.

WHAT I AM TRYING TO EXPRESS, IN SLIGHTLY OBTUSE TERMS, IS SIMPLY THAT

....
PLAINLY STATE THE ERROR YOU MADE

"I WAS WRONG"

TO SAY THAT. LET THE

I MUST ADMIT, IT FEELS ....
DESCRIPTION OF YOUR PRESENT EMOTIONAL STATE

RECORD SHOW ....
SOMETHING TRUTHFUL

IN RETROSPECT, MY MISTAKE WAS SO OBVIOUS THAT ONLY A

COMMON FOOL WOULD MAKE IT — I SHOULD NEVER HAVE

.... WHILE WE MAY
EXPLAIN HOW YOU CAME TO MAKE SUCH A GRIEVOUS ERROR

NEVER KNOW THE FULL EXTENT OF MY INCORRECTNESS, I CAN

ASSURE YOU THAT I HAVE LEARNED MY LESSON. HENCEFORTH,

I WILL ALWAYS ....
SUCCINCTLY ENCAPSULATE THE LESSON YOU HAVE LEARNED

LEST YOU OR I LOSE ANY SLEEP OVER THE MATTER, I WISH TO

ASSURE YOU THAT I RECOGNIZE THE GRAVITY OF MY ERROR. I

ACKNOWLEDGE THE HORRIBLE SIDE EFFECTS, INCLUDING

....
THE CONSEQUENCES

(BUT NOT LIMITED TO)

WHILE I CAN NEVER PROPERLY REVERSE THE DAMAGES, TO

MAKE IT UP TO YOU I WISH TO ....
AN OFFERED ACT OF RESTITUTION

THOUGH IT IS BUT A PIDDLING GESTURE BORN OUT OF GUILT,

IT IS THE BEST I CAN DO CONSIDERING THE CIRCUMSTANCES.

THANK YOU FOR YOUR GRACIOUS PARDONS, AND FOR BEING SO

DISCRETE AS TO NOT MENTION MY FALLIBILITY TO ANYONE.

SINCERELY, ...
NAME OF SENDER

APPLY STRIP OF ADHESIVE HERE

THE BUREAU OF COMMUNICATION

BUREAU OF · COMMUNICATION · EST. 1860

FORMAL NOTICE

RECORD OF INCORRECTNESS

STEP TWO
NEATLY WRITE THE
NAME AND ADDRESS
OF RECIPIENT HERE

AFFIX
POSTAGE
IN THIS
SPACE

ADD ANOTHER ADHESIVE STRIP HERE

BUREAUCRATIC FEEDBACK

BUREAU OF COMMUNICATION · EST. 1860

FORM **Z-123**

FILING DATE

DOCUMENTED OPINIONS

DEAR BUREAU OF COMMUNICATION, I WISH TO OFFER THE FOLLOWING FEEDBACK: YOUR FORMS ARE QUITE

.... AND ....
ADJECTIVE   ADJECTIVE

I WOULD RATE THIS BOOK A " .... ". IN THE FUTURE YOU
LETTER GRADE

MIGHT WANT TO CONSIDER: ....
SUGGESTED IMPROVEMENT

ALSO, YOU SHOULD HAVE LESS ....
SOMETHING TO REMOVE

AND MORE .... IN THE BOOK. AND

WHILE YOU ARE AT IT, I THINK YOU REALLY OUGHT TO

....
MORE IDEAS, BOTH GOOD AND BAD

ADDITIONAL THOUGHTS

....

....

SURVEY
BECAUSE, WE ARE TOO CURIOUS FOR OUR OWN GOOD

☐ I HAVE MAILED FORMS   ☐ I READ THEM LIKE A BOOK

I AM A ☐ MAN ☐ WOMAN ☐ CHILD, AGED: ....

YOUR E-MAIL ADDRESS: ....

BOOK ACQUIRED:
☐ IN A STORE
☐ VIA THE INTERNET
☐ AS A GIFT
☐ THROUGH THEFT

I LEARNED OF IT:
....
....

I AM A:
☐ DISGRUNTLED FAN
☐ TERRIBLE PERSON
☐ RAVING LUNATIC
☐ FAMILY MEMBER

RATE THIS BOOK:
☐ AWFUL
☐ TERRIBLE
☐ RATHER POOR
☐ ABYSMAL
☐ ATROCIOUS
☐ STUPID
☐ ANNOYING
☐ NOT FUNNY
☐ UGLY
☐ CONFUSING
☐ BROKEN

SUGGEST A NEW FORM:
....

RATE THE WRITING OF THE FORMS:
TOO SERIOUS - RELATIVELY PERFECT - TOO SILLY
◯ ◯ ◯ ◯ ◯ ◯ ◯

RATE THE AUTHORS OF THIS BOOK:
TOO HANDSOME — A GOOD MIX — TOO SMART
◯ ◯ ◯ ◯ ◯ ◯ ◯

I SOLEMNLY SWEAR TO PROMOTE THE B.o.C.

THE BUREAU OF COMMUNICATION

BUREAU OF COMMUNICATION
EST. 1860
COMMUNICATION

FORMAL NOTICE
BUREAUCRATIC FEEDBACK

WRITE THE NAME
OF SENDER HERE

BUREAU OF COMMUNICATION
Magnetism Studios
P.O. BOX 250209
NEW YORK, N.Y.
10025

AFFIX
POSTAGE
IN THIS
SPACE